P · O · C · K · E · T · S

ESSENTIAL
FACTS

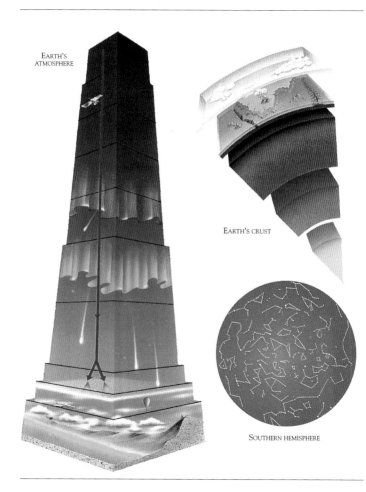

EARTH'S ATMOSPHERE

EARTH'S CRUST

SOUTHERN HEMISPHERE

P · O · C · K · E · T · S

ESSENTIAL
FACTS

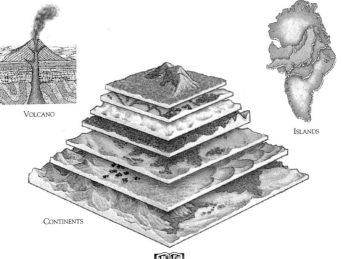

VOLCANO

ISLANDS

CONTINENTS

DORLING KINDERSLEY

London • New York • Sydney • Moscow

www.dk.com

A DORLING KINDERSLEY BOOK

www.dk.com

Project editors	Tim Hetherington
	Esther Labi
	Martin Redfern
Designer	Janet Allis
Art editor	Clair Watson
Design assistant	Andrea Jeffrey-Hall
Senior editor	Alastair Dougall
Senior art editor	Sarah Crouch
Picture research	Sam Ruston
Production	Josie Alabaster
	Katie Holmes

First published in Great Britain in 1996
by Dorling Kindersley Limited
9 Henrietta Street, Covent Garden, London WC2E 8PS

2 4 6 8 10 9 7 5 3 1

A CIP catalogue record for this book is available from
the British Library

ISBN 0 7513 3031 0

Colour reproduction by Colourscan, Singapore
Printed and bound in Italy by L.E.G.O.

CONTENTS

How to use this book 8

THE WORLD AROUND US   10
The night sky 12
The Sun and Moon 14
The planets 16
Planet Earth 18
World time zones 22
The physical world 24
Water 26
The Earth's crust 28
World climate zones 30

THE POLITICAL WORLD 32
The political world 34
The world's nations 38
American states 48
World resources 50

Rulers and leaders 52
Major wars 58

TECHNOLOGY 60
Transport milestones 62
Road and rail 64
Sea and air 66
Communications 68
Engineering 70
The electronic brain 72

SCIENCE 74
Scientific milestones 76
The periodic table 78
Scientific units 80
Light and sound 82
Food and nutrition 84

MATHEMATICS 86
Number systems 88
Arithmetic 90
Geometry 92
Angles and circles 94
Weights and measures 96
Conversion tables 98
Speed 100

PEOPLE 102
The human body 104
The spoken word 106
The written word 108
Faith systems 110
Sport 112
The arts 114
Calendars 120

INDEX 122

HOW TO USE THIS BOOK

These pages show you how to use *Pockets: Essential Facts*. The book is divided into six sections. These cover all the essential subjects, ranging from the solar system, to world religion, to mathematics. At the beginning of each section there is a picture page and a guide to the contents of that particular section.

HEADING
The heading describes the overall subject of the page. This page is about water.

INTRODUCTION
The introduction provides an overview of the subject. After reading this, you should have a clear idea of what the following page, or pages, are about.

Corner coding

Heading

Introduction

Annotation

Label

Table

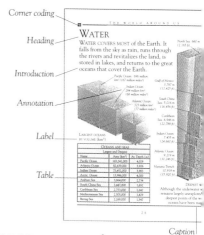

THE WORLD AROUND US

WATER

WATER COVERS MOST of the Earth. It falls from the sky as rain, runs through the rivers and revitalizes the land, is stored in lakes, and returns to the great oceans that cover the Earth.

Pacific Ocean: 696 million km³ (167 million miles³)

Indian Ocean: 284 million km³ (68 million miles³)

Gulf of Mexico: 2,332 m (12,425 ft)

South China Sea: 5,016 m (16,456 ft)

Caribbean Sea: 6,946 m (22,788 ft)

Indian Ocean: 7,455 m (24,460 ft)

North Sea: 660 m (2,165 ft)

LARGEST OCEANS BY VOLUME (km³)

Atlantic Ocean: 9,219 m (30,246 ft)

Mariana Trench: 10,924 m (35,820 ft)

OCEANS AND SEAS		
	Largest and Deepest	
Name	Area (km²)	Av. Depth (m)
Pacific Ocean	165,241,000	4,028
Atlantic Ocean	82,439,000	3,926
Indian Ocean	73,452,000	3,963
Arctic Ocean	13,986,000	4,000
Arabian Sea	3,864,000	2,734
South China Sea	3,447,000	1,652
Caribbean Sea	2,753,000	2,647
Mediterranean Sea	2,505,000	1,429
Bering Sea	2,269,000	1,547

DEEPEST
Although the underwater remains largely unexplored, deepest points of the oceans have been measured.

2.6

CORNER CODING
The corners of the main section pages are colour coded to remind you which section you are in.

THE WORLD AROUND US

THE POLITICAL WORLD

TECHNOLOGY

SCIENCE

MATHEMATICS

PEOPLE

CAPTIONS AND ANNOTATIONS
Each illustration carries an explanatory caption. Some also have annotations, in *italics*. These point out the features of an illustration, and often use leader lines.

LABELS
For clarity, some pictures have labels. These give extra information about the picture, or may provide clearer identification.

RUNNING HEADS
These remind you which section you are in. The top of the left-hand page gives the section name, and the top of the right-hand page gives the subject heading.

FACT BOXES
Many pages have fact boxes. These provide at-a-glance information about the subject, such as how much water flows from the Amazon.

MAPS
Some pages in the book contain maps. These have annotations and labels to aid identification and give further information.

Fact box

Running head

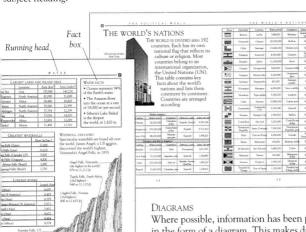

DIAGRAMS
Where possible, information has been presented in the form of a diagram. This makes data more accessible and easier to absorb. On these pages, for example, the volumes of the greatest oceans are shown as an illustration.

TABLES
Tables give comparative data listings for particular subject examples. On these pages, the relative sizes of aquatic features are listed in numerical order.

INDEX
At the back of the book, there is an index. It lists alphabetically every subject included in the book. By referring to the index, information on particular topics can be found.

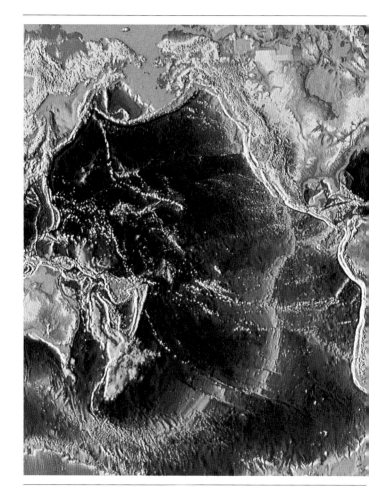

THE WORLD AROUND US

THE NIGHT SKY 12
THE SUN AND MOON 14
THE PLANETS 16
PLANET EARTH 18
WORLD TIME ZONES 22
THE PHYSICAL WORLD 24
WATER 26
THE EARTH'S CRUST 28
WORLD CLIMATE ZONES 30

THE NIGHT SKY

STARS, OF WHICH OUR SUN is an example, are scattered throughout the Universe. Ancient people observed their patterns in the night sky as different groups, or constellations. For thousands of years, navigators have used the stars as guides.

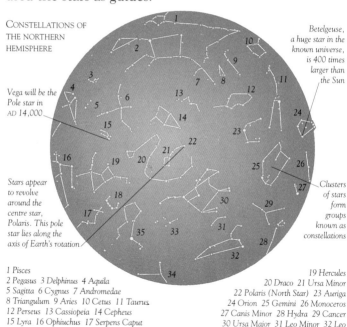

CONSTELLATIONS OF THE NORTHERN HEMISPHERE

Betelgeuse, a huge star in the known universe, is 400 times larger than the Sun

Vega will be the Pole star in AD 14,000

Stars appear to revolve around the centre star, Polaris. This pole star lies along the axis of Earth's rotation

Clusters of stars form groups known as constellations

1 Pisces
2 Pegasus 3 Delphinus 4 Aquila
5 Sagitta 6 Cygnus 7 Andromedae
8 Triangulum 9 Aries 10 Cetus 11 Taurus
12 Perseus 13 Cassiopeia 14 Cepheus
15 Lyra 16 Ophiuchus 17 Serpens Caput
18 Corona Borealis

19 Hercules
20 Draco 21 Ursa Minor
22 Polaris (North Star) 23 Auriga
24 Orion 25 Gemini 26 Monoceros
27 Canis Minor 28 Hydra 29 Cancer
30 Ursa Major 31 Leo Minor 32 Leo
33 Canes Venatici 34 Virgo 35 Boötes

THE MILKY WAY

The Sun is one of the 200 billion stars in our galaxy, the Milky Way. Scientists believe we belong to a spiral-style galaxy with a diameter of 100,000 light years. Because of the solar system's position in the Orion arm of the spiral, we view the Milky Way as a luminous band of bright stars, without the spiral details.

MILKY WAY WITH METEOR STREAK   Milky Way

CONSTELLATIONS OF
THE SOUTHERN
HEMISPHERE

Stars near the edge become visible month by month through the year

Sirius is the brightest star in the night sky

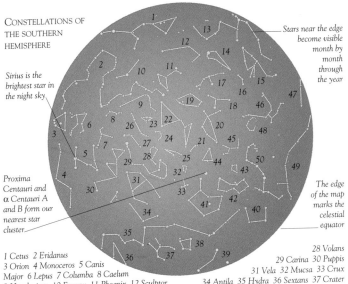

Proxima Centauri and α Centauri A and B form our nearest star cluster

The edge of the map marks the celestial equator

1 Cetus 2 Eridanus
3 Orion 4 Monoceros 5 Canis
Major 6 Lepus 7 Columba 8 Caelum
9 Horologium 10 Fornax 11 Phoenix 12 Sculptor
13 Aquarius 14 Piscis Austrinus 15 Capricornus
16 Microscopium 17 Grus 18 Indus 19 Tucana
20 Pavo 21 Apus 22 Hydrus 23 Reticulum
24 Mensa 25 Chameleon 26 Dorado 27 Pictor

28 Volans
29 Carina 30 Puppis
31 Vela 32 Mucsa 33 Crux
34 Antila 35 Hydra 36 Sextans 37 Crater
38 Corvus 39 Virgo 40 Libra 41 Centaurus
42 Lupus 43 Norma 44 Triangulum Australe
45 Ara 46 Sagittarius 47 Aquila 48 Corona
Australis 49 Ophiuchus 50 Scorpius

THE SUN AND MOON

OUR CLOSEST STAR, the Sun, is a spinning ball of gas. Nuclear reactions take place in its core, creating heat and light. The Moon revolves around Earth in its orbit of the Sun.

THE SUN

- Diameter: 1,392,000 km (865,000 miles)
- Time taken to orbit galaxy: 240 million years
- Distance from Earth: 149.6 million km (93 million miles)
- Surface temperature: 5,500°C (9,900°F)
- Life expectancy: 10 billion years
- Age: 5 billion years
- Mass (Earth =1): 332,946

WHAT IS A SOLAR ECLIPSE? Occasionally the Moon becomes precisely aligned between the Sun and the Earth. Viewed from parts of the Earth, the Moon covers the disc of the Sun perfectly. This blocks the light and causes a brief period of darkness known as a solar eclipse.

TOTAL SOLAR ECLIPSES (1999–2009)	
DATE	WHERE VISIBLE
11 Aug 1999	N Atlantic, N Europe, Middle East, N India
21 June 2001	S America, S Atlantic, S Africa, Pacific
4 Dec 2002	Mid-Atlantic, S Africa, S Pacific, Australia
23 Nov 2003	S Pacific, Antarctic
8 Apr 2005	Pacific, Panama, Venezuela
29 Mar 2006	Atlantic, Libya, Turkey, Russia
1 Aug 2008	Greenland, Russia, China
22 Jul 2009	India, China, Pacific

SOLAR ECLIPSE

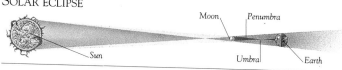

Moon   Penumbra

Sun   Umbra   Earth

THE MOON, AS SEEN FROM SPACE

THE MOON

- Diameter: 3,476 km (2,160 miles)
- Age: 4.6 billion years
- Distance from Earth: 384,000 km (238,000 miles)
- Surface temperature: –155°C / 105°C (–247/221°F)
- The Moon spins on its axis at the same rate that it orbits the Earth, so the same side is always visible.
- The pull of the Moon's gravity is largely responsible for the rise and fall of tides on Earth.

THE PHASES OF THE MOON

| NEW MOON | CRESCENT | FIRST QUARTER | GIBBOUS | FULL MOON | GIBBOUS | LAST QUARTER | CRESCENT |

WHAT IS A LUNAR ECLIPSE?

Occasionally the Earth becomes perfectly aligned between the Sun and the Moon. When this happens, the Earth blocks light from the Sun and cast its shadow across the Moon. Viewed from Earth, this shadow crossing the Moon is known as a lunar eclipse.

TOTAL LUNAR ECLIPSES (1999–2009)	
DATE	WHERE VISIBLE
21 Jan 2000	N America, parts of S America, SW Europe
16 July 2000	Pacific, Australia, SE Asia
9 Jan 2001	Europe, Asia, Africa
16 May 2003	N America, C and S America, Europe, Africa
9 Nov 2003	N America, C and S America, Africa, W Asia
4 May 2004	Europe, Africa, Asia
28 Oct 2004	N America, C and S America, Europe, Africa
3 Mar 2007	Africa, Europe, Middle East
28 Aug 2007	Pacific, E Australia, Alaska
21 Feb 2008	N America, S America, W Europe, W Africa

LUNAR ECLIPSE

Earth Umbra Penumbra

Sun

Moon

THE PLANETS

Jupiter, the largest planet, could contain 1,300 Earths

A PLANET IS A BODY that orbits the Sun or any other star. The nine planets in our solar system divide into two groups. Mercury, Venus, Earth, and Mars form the dense and rocky inner planets. Jupiter, Saturn, Uranus, Neptune, and Pluto belong to the gaseous or icy outer ones.

Mercury has the fastest orbiting speed around the Sun

VENUS

MARS

EARTH

MERCURY

Venus has thick clouds of sulphuric acid

The planet's red colour is caused by iron oxide

JUPITER

Inner and outer planets are separated by an asteroid belt

Sun   Earth

Mercury Venus   Mars   Jupiter   Saturn

INNER PLANETS				
	MERCURY	VENUS	EARTH	MARS
DISTANCE FROM THE SUN IN MILLION KM (MILLION MILES)	57.9 (36.0)	108.2 (67.2)	149.6 (93)	227.9 (141.6)
DIAMETER IN KM (MILES)	4,878 (3,031)	12,103 (7,520)	12,756 (7,926)	6,786 (4,217)
TIME TAKEN TO ORBIT THE SUN	87.97 DAYS	224.70 DAYS	365.26 DAYS	686.98 DAYS
TIME TAKEN TO TURN ON AXIS	58 DAYS 16 HOURS	243 DAYS 14 HOURS	23 HOURS 56 MINS	24 HOURS 37 MINS
SURFACE TEMPERATURE	−180 - 430°C (−292 - 806°F)	465°C (869°F)	−70 - 55°C (−94 - 131°F)	−120 - 25°C (−184 - 77°F)
NUMBER OF MOONS	NONE	NONE	1	2
MASS (EARTH = 1)	0.055	0.81	1	2
DENSITY (WATER = 1)	5.43	5.25	5.52	3.95

Saturn has at least 18 moons – more than any other planet

NEPTUNE

PLUTO

Neptune has winds of up to 2,000 km/h (1,240 mph)

URANUS

Uranus has the most tilted axis of all the planets – 98° to the vertical

Pluto is the smallest, darkest, and coldest planet. It is the only outer planet made of solid material

SATURN

Saturn's rings consist of ice-covered rock and dust particles. Saturn has the lowest density of all the planets: set on a huge lake, it would float

PLANETARY ORBITS
The Sun's huge gravitational pull holds the solar system together, forcing the planets to circle the Sun. The orbits of the four inner planets lie close to the Sun. Mercury, the nearest planet to the Sun, is 100 times closer than Pluto.

Uranus

Neptune

Pluto

OUTER PLANETS				
JUPITER	SATURN	URANUS	NEPTUNE	PLUTO
778.3 (483.6)	1,427 (886)	2,871 (1,784)	4,497 (2,794)	5,914 (3,675)
142,984 (88,846)	120,536 (74,898)	51,118 (31,763)	49,528 (30,775)	2,284 (1,419)
11.86 YEARS	29.46 YEARS	84.01 YEARS	164.79 YEARS	248.54 YEARS
9 HOURS 55 MINS	10 HOURS 40 MINS	17 HOURS 14 MINS	16 HOURS 7 MINS	6 DAYS 9 HOURS
–150°C (–238°F) AT CLOUD TOPS	–180°C (–292°F) AT CLOUD TOPS	–210°C (–346°F) AT CLOUD TOPS	–210°C (–346°F) AT CLOUD TOPS	–220°C (–364°F)
16	18	15	8	1
318	95.18	14.5	17.14	0.0022
1.33	0.69	1.29	1.64	2.03

PLANET EARTH

OF ALL THE PLANETS, only the Earth has the necessary ingredients for life. Because of its unique position in the solar system, all aspects of the environment are regulated, from the seasonal cycles to the oceans tides.

THE SEASONS
The Earth orbits the Sun with a tilt of 23.5°. This mechanism causes a rotation of seasons. When the northern hemisphere tilts towards the Sun, it experiences summer, and the south, winter. As the orbit changes, so the seasons change.

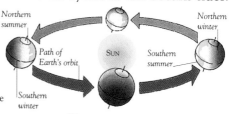

Northern summer

Path of Earth's orbit

SUN

Northern winter

Southern summer

Southern winter

THE EARTH

- Diameter: 12,756 km (7,926 miles) at equator, 12,713 km (7,899 miles) at poles
- Age: 4.6 billion years old
- Distance from the Sun: 149.6 million km (93 million miles)
- Mass: 5,854 billion billion tonnes
- Area: 29.2% land, 70.8% water
- Orbiting time: 365.26 days
- Orbiting speed: 29.8 km /sec (18.5 miles/sec)

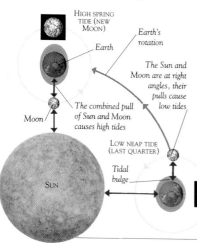

HIGH SPRING TIDE (NEW MOON)

Earth

Earth's rotation

The Sun and Moon are at right angles, their pulls cause low tides

Moon

The combined pull of Sun and Moon causes high tides

LOW NEAP TIDE (LAST QUARTER)

Tidal bulge

SUN

HOW TIDES ARE FORMED
Gravity from the Sun and Moon causes the cycle of ocean tides on Earth. High, low, and neap tides all result when configurations of the Sun and Moon pull on the rotating Earth.

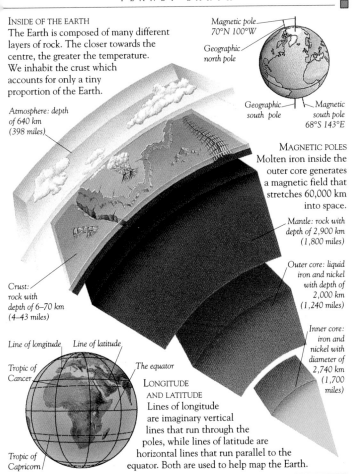

INSIDE OF THE EARTH

The Earth is composed of many different layers of rock. The closer towards the centre, the greater the temperature. We inhabit the crust which accounts for only a tiny proportion of the Earth.

Magnetic pole 70°N 100°W

Geographic north pole

Geographic south pole

Magnetic south pole 68°S 143°E

Atmosphere: depth of 640 km (398 miles)

MAGNETIC POLES

Molten iron inside the outer core generates a magnetic field that stretches 60,000 km into space.

Mantle: rock with depth of 2,900 km (1,800 miles)

Outer core: liquid iron and nickel with depth of 2,000 km (1,240 miles)

Crust: rock with depth of 6–70 km (4–43 miles)

Inner core: iron and nickel with diameter of 2,740 km (1,700 miles)

Line of longitude   Line of latitude

Tropic of Cancer

The equator

LONGITUDE AND LATITUDE

Lines of longitude are imaginary vertical lines that run through the poles, while lines of latitude are horizontal lines that run parallel to the equator. Both are used to help map the Earth.

Tropic of Capricorn

More about the Earth

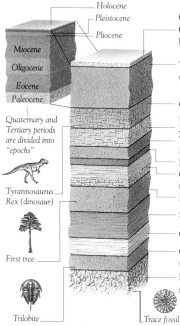

Holocene
Pleistocene
Pliocene

Miocene
Oligocene
Eocene
Paleocene

Quaternary and Tertiary periods are divided into "epochs"

Tyrannosaurus Rex (dinosaur)

First tree

Trilobite

Trace fossil

GEOLOGICAL TIME SCALE

Quaternary (2 MYA): Ice ages in the north; humans emerge.

Tertiary (65 MYA): the continents take shape; mammals and birds replace dinosaurs.

Cretaceous (146 MYA): South America and Africa split; dinosaurs die out.

Jurassic (208 MYA): the age of the dinosaurs.

Triassic (245 MYA): Earth's one land mass, Pangaea, splits into Gondwanaland and Laurasia.

Permian (290 MYA): first reptiles.

Carboniferous (363 MYA): swampy tropical forests in the north.

Devonian (409 MYA): early land plants appear.

Silurian (439 MYA): most life exists in the sea.

Ordovician (510 MYA): molluscs appear.

Cambrian (570 MYA): life forms exist in the sea.

Precambrian (4,600 MYA): few fossils survive from this period.

THE GREENHOUSE EFFECT

Pollutant gases, such as carbon dioxide, act like glass in a greenhouse. They let the Sun's rays in but prevent excess heat from escaping the Earth's surface. This process, known as global warming, can cause temperatures to rise. Scientists predict that the temperature on Earth could rise by as much as 4°C (7°F) by the year 2050.

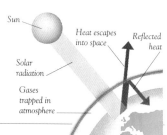

Sun

Heat escapes into space

Reflected heat

Solar radiation

Gases trapped in atmosphere

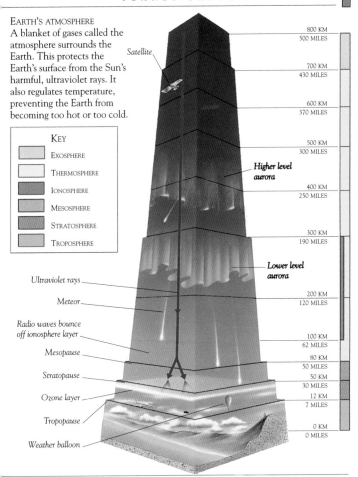

EARTH'S ATMOSPHERE
A blanket of gases called the atmosphere surrounds the Earth. This protects the Earth's surface from the Sun's harmful, ultraviolet rays. It also regulates temperature, preventing the Earth from becoming too hot or too cold.

Satellite

800 KM	500 MILES
700 KM	430 MILES
600 KM	370 MILES
500 KM	300 MILES
400 KM	250 MILES
300 KM	190 MILES
200 KM	120 MILES
100 KM	62 MILES
80 KM	50 MILES
50 KM	30 MILES
12 KM	7 MILES
0 KM	0 MILES

KEY

- EXOSPHERE
- THERMOSPHERE
- IONOSPHERE
- MESOSPHERE
- STRATOSPHERE
- TROPOSPHERE

Higher level aurora

Lower level aurora

Ultraviolet rays

Meteor

Radio waves bounce off ionosphere layer

Mesopause

Stratopause

Ozone layer

Tropopause

Weather balloon

2 1

WORLD TIME ZONES

THE EARTH IS divided into 24 time zones, one for each hour of the day. Greenwich, in southeast London, England, is on the 0° meridian. Time advances by one hour for every 15° of longitude east of Greenwich.

TIME ZONES
The numbers on the map indicate the number of hours that must be subtracted or added to reach GMT. When it is noon at Greenwich, for example, it is 10 p.m. in Sydney, Australia. Time zones are adjusted to regional administrative boundaries.

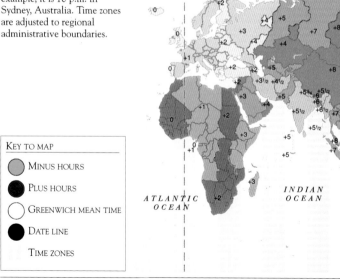

KEY TO MAP

🔵 MINUS HOURS

⚫ PLUS HOURS

⚪ GREENWICH MEAN TIME

⚫ DATE LINE

TIME ZONES

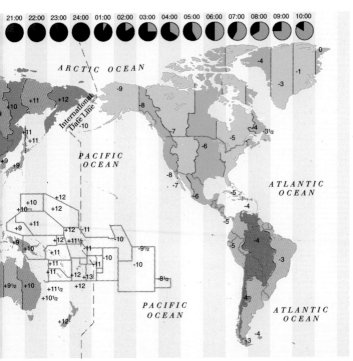

GMT
Greenwich Mean Time (GMT) is the exact time in Greenwich, London. Clocks are set depending on whether they are east or west of Greenwich.

INTERNATIONAL DATE LINE
The International Date Line is an imaginary line that runs along the 180° meridian but deviates around countries.

21:00 22:00 23:00 24:00 01:00 02:00 03:00 04:00 05:00 06:00 07:00 08:00 09:00 10:00

ARCTIC OCEAN

International Date Line

PACIFIC OCEAN

ATLANTIC OCEAN

PACIFIC OCEAN

ATLANTIC OCEAN

THE PHYSICAL WORLD

LAND ACCOUNTS FOR just over a quarter of the Earth's total surface area. This comprises seven principal landmasses, known as the continents. Each continent features a variety of landscapes, such as mountains, deserts, forests, and pasturelands.

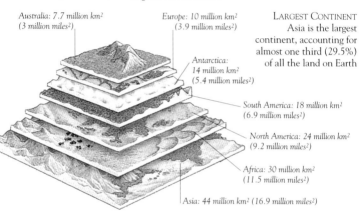

Australia: 7.7 million km²
(3 million miles²)

Europe: 10 million km²
(3.9 million miles²)

Antarctica:
14 million km²
(5.4 million miles²)

South America: 18 million km²
(6.9 million miles²)

North America: 24 million km²
(9.2 million miles²)

Africa: 30 million km²
(11.5 million miles²)

Asia: 44 million km² (16.9 million miles²)

LARGEST CONTINENT
Asia is the largest continent, accounting for almost one third (29.5%) of all the land on Earth

HIGH AND LOW POINTS AROUND THE WORLD				
NAME OF CONTINENT	HIGHEST POINT ABOVE SEA LEVEL	HEIGHT IN METRES (FEET)	LOWEST POINT BELOW SEA LEVEL	DEPTH IN METRES (FEET)
Asia	Mt Everest	8,848 (29,030)	Dead Sea	–400 (–1,312)
Africa	Kilimanjaro	5,895 (19,341)	Qattâra Depression	–133 (–436)
N America	Denali (Mt McKinley)	6,194 (20,323)	Death Valley	–86 (–282)
S America	Aconcagua	6,960 (22,836)	Peninsular Valdez	–40 (–131)
Antarctica	Vinson Massif	5,140 (16,864)	Bentley Subglacial Trench	–2,538 (–8,327)
Europe	Elbrus	5,642 (18,511)	Caspian Sea	–28 (–92)
Australia	Mt Kosciusko	2,228 (7,310)	Lake Eyre	–16 (–52)

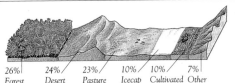

26% 24% 23% 10% 10% 7%
Forest Desert Pasture Icecap Cultivated Other

DIVISION OF THE EARTH'S LAND AREA

The total surface area of the Earth is about 510 million km², of which only 149 million km² is land. Of this, over half is either abundant forest or inhospitable desert.

LARGEST DESERTS	AREA IN KM² (MILES²)
Sahara Desert (Africa)	9,065,000 (3,500,000)
Arabian Desert (Asia)	1,300,000 (502,000)
Gobi Desert (Asia)	1,040,000 (402,000)
Kalahari Desert (Africa)	580,000 (224,000)
Great Sandy Desert (Australia)	414,000 (160,000)
Chihuahuan Desert (N America)	370,000 (143,000)
Takla Makan Desert (Asia)	320,000 (198,848)
Kara Kum Desert (Asia)	310,000 (120,000)
Namib Desert (Africa)	310,000 (120,000)
Thar Desert (Asia)	260,000 (100,000)

Borneo: 744,366 km²
(287,422 miles²)

Honshu, Japan:
230,448 km²
(88,983 miles²)

Greenland:
2,175,600 km²
(840,065 miles²)

LARGEST ISLANDS

Greenland is the world's largest island (Australia is considered a continent). It is three times as big as Borneo, the second largest island in the world, and nine times the size of Honshu, Japan's largest island.

HIGHEST MOUNTAINS

The 10 highest peaks are all found in the Himalaya mountain range, which lies between Tibet/China and the Indian subcontinent.

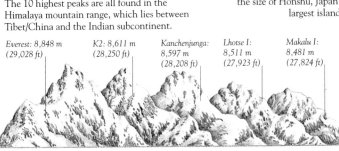

Everest: 8,848 m
(29,028 ft)

K2: 8,611 m
(28,250 ft)

Kanchenjunga:
8,597 m
(28,208 ft)

Lhotse I:
8,511 m
(27,923 ft)

Makalu I:
8,481 m
(27,824 ft)

WATER

WATER COVERS MOST of the Earth. It falls from the sky as rain, runs through the rivers and revitalizes the land, is stored in lakes, and returns to the great oceans that cover the Earth.

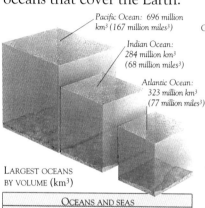

Pacific Ocean: 696 million km³ (167 million miles³)

Indian Ocean: 284 million km³ (68 million miles³)

Atlantic Ocean: 323 million km³ (77 million miles³)

LARGEST OCEANS BY VOLUME (km³)

North Sea: 660 m (2,165 ft)

Gulf of Mexico: 3,787 m (12,425 ft)

South China Sea: 5,016 m (16,456 ft)

Caribbean Sea: 6,946 m (22,788 ft)

Indian Ocean: 7,455 m (24,660 ft)

Atlantic Ocean: 9,219 m (30,246 ft)

Mariana Trench: 10,918 m (35,820 ft)

DEEPEST WATER
Although the underwater world remains largely unexplored, the deepest points of the world's oceans have been mapped.

OCEANS AND SEAS		
Largest and Deepest		
Name	Area (km²)	Av. Depth (m)
Pacific Ocean	165,241,000	4,028
Atlantic Ocean	82,439,000	3,926
Indian Ocean	73,452,000	3,963
Arctic Ocean	13,986,000	4,000
Arabian Sea	3,864,000	2,734
South China Sea	3,447,000	1,652
Caribbean Sea	2,753,000	2,647
Mediterranean Sea	2,505,000	1,429
Bering Sea	2,269,000	1,547

LARGEST LAKES AND INLAND SEAS

Lake	Location	Area (km²)	Area (miles²)
Caspian Sea	Asia	370,980	143,236
Lake Superior	North America	82,098	31,698
Lake Victoria	Africa	69,480	26,826
Lake Huron	North America	59,566	22,999
Lake Michigan	North America	57,754	22,299
Aral Sea	Asia	37,056	14,307
Lake Tanganyika	Africa	32,891	12,699
Lake Baikal	Siberia	31,498	12,161

WATER FACTS

• Oceans represent 94% of the Earth's water.

• The Amazon flows into the ocean at a rate of 18,000 m³ per second.

• Siberia's Lake Baikal is the deepest lake in the world, at 1,620 m.

GREATEST WATERFALLS

Name	Flow (m³/sec)
Boyoma Falls (Zaire)	17,000
Khône Falls (Laos)	11,610
Niagara Falls (Canada/ US)	5,830
Grande Falls (Uruguay)	4,500
Paulo Afonso Falls (Brazil)	2,890
Urubupungá Falls (Brazil)	2,750

LONGEST RIVERS

Name	Length (km)
Nile (Africa)	6,695
Amazon (S America)	6,439
Yangtze (Asia)	6,379
Mississippi-Missouri (N America)	5,971
Ob-Irtysh (Asia)	5,410
Yellow (Asia)	4,672
Amur (Asia)	4,464
Congo (Africa)	4,374

WATERFALL DISCOVERY
Spectacular waterfalls are found all over the world. James Angel, a US aviator, discovered the world's highest, Venezuela's Angel Falls, in 1935.

Angel Falls, Venezuela (the highest in the world) : 979 m (3,212 ft)

Tugela Falls, South Africa (2nd highest) : 948 m (3,110 ft)

Utigård Falls, Norway (3rd highest): 800 m (2,625 ft)

Yosemite Falls, US (4th highest): 739 m (2,425 ft)

Khône Falls, Laos (the world's widest waterfall): 10.8 km (6.7 miles)

THE EARTH'S CRUST

A LAYER OF ROCK known as the crust covers the Earth. Huge slabs called tectonic plates join to form this protective layer. Movement occurs where these plates meet, and this may cause volcanoes, mountains, deep-sea trenches, fault lines, and earthquakes to develop.

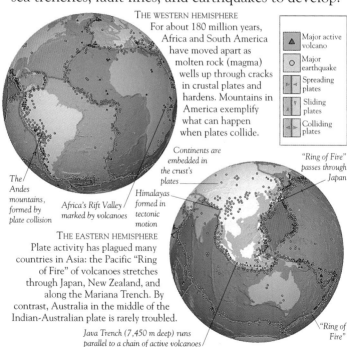

THE WESTERN HEMISPHERE
For about 180 million years, Africa and South America have moved apart as molten rock (magma) wells up through cracks in crustal plates and hardens. Mountains in America exemplify what can happen when plates collide.

▲	Major active volcano
○	Major earthquake
▶◀	Spreading plates
▼	Sliding plates
◀▶	Colliding plates

The Andes mountains, formed by plate collision

Africa's Rift Valley marked by volcanoes

Continents are embedded in the crust's plates

Himalayas formed in tectonic motion

"Ring of Fire" passes through Japan

THE EASTERN HEMISPHERE
Plate activity has plagued many countries in Asia: the Pacific "Ring of Fire" of volcanoes stretches through Japan, New Zealand, and along the Mariana Trench. By contrast, Australia in the middle of the Indian-Australian plate is rarely troubled.

Java Trench (7,450 m deep) runs parallel to a chain of active volcanoes

"Ring of Fire"

MAJOR ACTIVE VOLCANOES		
NAME	HEIGHT(M)	LAST ERUPTION
Nyamuragira, Zaire	3,053	1989
Mt Cameroon, Cameroon	4,070	1982
Erebus, Antarctica	3,794	1989
Kliuchevskoi, Siberia	4,850	1990
Ruapehu, New Zealand	2,796	1989
Etna, Sicily, Italy	3,350	1992
Stromboli, Italy	926	1990
Mount St Helens, US	2,549	1988
Mauna Loa, Hawaii	4,170	1984
Sangay, Ecuador	5,230	1989
Popocatepetl, Mexico	5,465	1943
Llullaillaco, Chile	6,723	1877

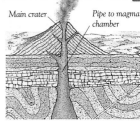

Main crater   *Pipe to magma chamber*

VOLCANO
Disturbances in the Earth's crust can provoke volcanic activity. This can force eruptions to release molten rock from deep inside the Earth to the surface.

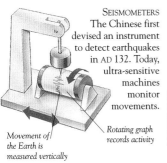

SEISMOMETERS
The Chinese first devised an instrument to detect earthquakes in AD 132. Today, ultra-sensitive machines monitor movements.

Movement of the Earth is measured vertically

Rotating graph records activity

MERCALLI AND RICHTER SCALES
Scientists measure the size of an earthquake using two different scales. The Richter scale is logarithmic and measures magnitude; and the Modified Mercalli Intensity scale measures the actual effect on a descriptive scale of I–XII.

MERCALLI SCALE

XII	Total destruction; waves seen on ground surface; river courses altered.
XI	Railway tracks bend; roads break up; large cracks appear in ground; rock falls.
X	Most buildings destroyed; water thrown from rivers; large landslides.
IX	General panic; damage to foundations; large buildings collapse.
VIII	Car steering affected; chimneys fall; tree branches break.
VII	Difficult for people to stand; plaster, bricks, and tiles fall.
VI	People walk unsteadily; windows break; pictures fall.
V	Doors swing open; buildings tremble; small objects fall.
IV	Dishes rattle; standing cars rock; trees shake.
III	Vibrations felt indoors; hanging objects swing.
II	People may notice slight vibrations.
I	Vibrations recorded by instruments.

1   2   3   4   5   6   7   8 8.9

RICHTER SCALE

WORLD CLIMATE ZONES

THE MAIN INFLUENCES on an area's climate are its distance from a large body of water, its height above sea level, and its distance from the equator. Climate is usually classified according to rainfall and temperature. Both sunlight levels and rainfall are highest, and show least variation, at the equator.

POLAR
In polar regions, all water is frozen solid. Antarctica contains more than 80% of the world's fresh water as ice. The coldest temperature ever recorded here is −57.8°C (−72°F).

COOL
Polar air fronts bring cold temperatures over the mainland. Large areas of North America, Northern Europe, and Russia/Siberia produce coniferous forests (taiga) that reflect this cool climate.

TEMPERATE
Hot, dry summers and damp winters characterize the temperate climates of mid-latitude areas. Warm and moist westerly winds affect these areas most of the year.

Equatorial forests contain 50% of all plant and animal species

The Atacama Desert, Chile, has an average of only 0.51 mm (0.02 in) of rain a year

The average temperature of Manaus, Brazil, is 27°C (68°F)

DESERT AND DRY LANDS
Deserts have the driest and most extreme climate in the world. Cold ocean currents or warm and dry subsiding air both reduce rainfall. Areas in a rainshadow or far from the sea are also prone to desertification.

TROPICAL
Tropical climates are hot: average noon-day temperatures vary by only 2°C (3.7°F). Large rainforests depend on rainfall all year round, while tropical grasslands like the African Savannah survive through dry and wet seasons.

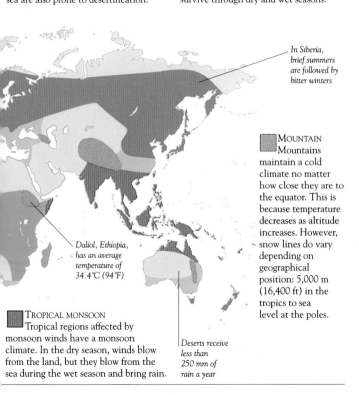

In Siberia, brief summers are followed by bitter winters

MOUNTAIN
Mountains maintain a cold climate no matter how close they are to the equator. This is because temperature decreases as altitude increases. However, snow lines do vary depending on geographical position: 5,000 m (16,400 ft) in the tropics to sea level at the poles.

Daliol, Ethiopia, has an average temperature of 34.4°C (94°F)

TROPICAL MONSOON
Tropical regions affected by monsoon winds have a monsoon climate. In the dry season, winds blow from the land, but they blow from the sea during the wet season and bring rain.

Deserts receive less than 250 mm of rain a year

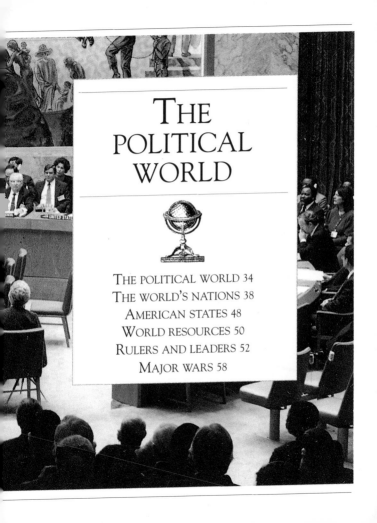

THE POLITICAL WORLD

THE POLITICAL WORLD 34
THE WORLD'S NATIONS 38
AMERICAN STATES 48
WORLD RESOURCES 50
RULERS AND LEADERS 52
MAJOR WARS 58

THE POLITICAL WORLD

POLITICS IS THE SCIENCE of social organization. Every country in the world has a system of government that controls society and makes representative decisions. However, countries may have different political systems that reflect various methods of government, such as democracies, communist states, or military dictatorships.

MOST POPULATED COUNTRIES	
COUNTRY	TOTAL (MILLIONS)
China	1,234.3
India	953.0
US	265.8
Indonesia	200.6
Brazil	164.4
Russia	146.7
Pakistan	144.5

LEAST POPULATED COUNTRIES	
COUNTRY	TOTAL
Vatican City	1000
Tuvalu	9,000
Nauru	11,000
Palau	16,500
San Marino	25,000
Liechtenstein	31,000
Monaco	31,000

This map shows population figures for the world's main land areas. It also shows the world's eight most populous cities.

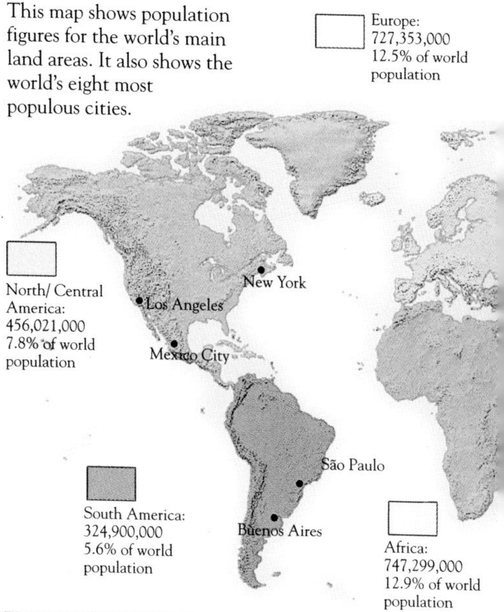

Europe:
727,353,000
12.5% of world population

North/ Central America:
456,021,000
7.8% of world population

New York

Los Angeles

Mexico City

São Paulo

Buenos Aires

South America:
324,900,000
5.6% of world population

Africa:
747,299,000
12.9% of world population

LARGEST COUNTRIES		
COUNTRY	AREA/MILLION KM²	MIL. MILES²
Russian Fed	17.40	6.59
Canada	9.97	3.85
China	9.40	3.64
US	9.37	3.62
Brazil	8.51	3.29

SMALLEST COUNTRIES		
COUNTRY	AREA/ KM²	MILES²
Vatican City	0.44	0.17
Monaco	1.95	0.75
Nauru	21.2	8.2
Tuvalu	26.0	10.0
San Marino	59.6	23.0

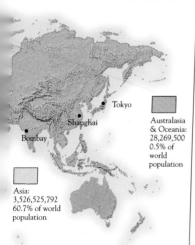

Tokyo

Shanghai

Bombay

Australasia & Oceania: 28,269,500 0.5% of world population

Asia: 3,526,525,792 60.7% of world population

WORLD ORGANIZATIONS

UNITED NATIONS
The United Nations (UN) was set up in 1945 to address and resolve global issues.

COMMONWEALTH
An association of ex-British sovereign states, its aims are mutually beneficial.

EUROPEAN UNION
This community of 15 principal states seeks economic union in Europe.

NATO
After World War II, the Allies created a joint military force for mutual purposes.

WHO
The World Health Organization monitors the well-being of all people.

UNESCO
This is the UN's educational, scientific, and cultural foundation.

RED CROSS
Founded in 1864, the society offers humanitarian aid to all those in need.

RED CRESCENT
The Islamic branch of the Red Cross works in Islamic countries.

Map of the world

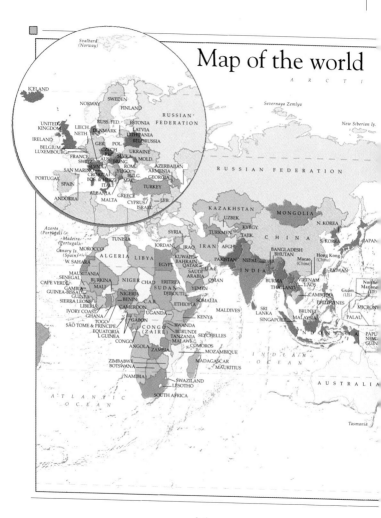

O C E A N

Queen Elizabeth Is.

Greenland
(Denmark)

ALASKA
(US)

Victoria Is.

Baffin Is.

C A N A D A

ATLANTIC
OCEAN

Aleutian Is. (US)

PACIFIC

OCEAN

UNITED STATES
OF AMERICA

Bermuda
(UK)

DOMINICAN REP.

Puerto Rico
(US)

Virgin Is.
(US)

British Virgin Is.
(UK)

BAHAMAS

Turks &
Caicos Is.
(UK)

Anguilla
(UK)

ANTIGUA &
BARBUDA

CUBA

Hawaii
(US)

Cayman Is.
(UK)
JAMAICA

ST KITTS & NEVIS
Montserrat (UK)
Aruba
(Neth.)

Guadeloupe
(France)

DOMINICA

Martinique
(France)

ST LUCIA

BARBADOS

MARSHALL IS.

MEXICO

BELIZE

HAITI

Netherlands Antilles
(Neth.)

GRENADA

ST VINCENT
& THE GRENADINES

Wallis & Futuna
(France)

GUATEMALA
EL SALVADOR
COSTA RICA

HONDURAS
NICARAGUA

TRINIDAD & TOBAGO

NAURU

K I R I B A T I

PANAMA

VEN.

French
Guiana
(France)

TUVALU

Tokelau
(NZ)

Cook Is.
(NZ)

COLOMBIA

GUYANA

SURINAM

American
Samoa
(US)

Niue
(NZ)

ECUADOR

B R A Z I L

FIJI

French Polynesia
(France)

PERU

VANUATU
SOLOMON IS.
New Caledonia
(France)

TONGA
WESTERN
SAMOA

Pitcairn Is.
(UK)

BOLIVIA

PARAGUAY

P A C I F I C

OCEAN

CHILE

ARGENTINA

URUGUAY

NEW ZEALAND

ATLANTIC

OCEAN

Falkland Is.
(UK)

South Georgia
(UK)

South Shetland Is.
(UK)

South Orkney Is.
(UK)

South
Sandwich Is.
(UK)

THE WORLD'S NATIONS

THE WORLD IS DIVIDED into 192 countries. Each has its own national flag that reflects its culture or religion. Most countries belong to an international organization, the United Nations (UN). This table contains key facts about the world's nations and lists them continent by continent. Countries are arranged according to land area.

UN HEADQUARTERS, NEW YORK

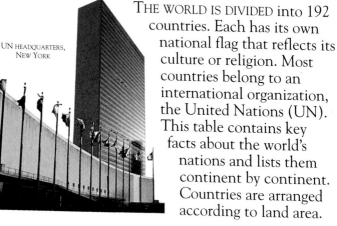

NORTH AMERICA						
FLAG	COUNTRY	CAPITAL	POPULATION	CURRENCY	OFFICIAL LANG.	AREA (SQ KM)
	Canada	Ottawa	29,800,000	Canadian dollar	English, French	9,976,140
	US	Washington DC	265,800,000	United States dollar	English	9,372,610
	Mexico	Mexico City	95,500,000	Mexican new peso	Spanish	1,958,200
CENTRAL AND SOUTH AMERICA						
FLAG	COUNTRY	CAPITAL	POPULATION	CURRENCY	OFFICIAL LANG.	AREA (SQ KM)
	Brazil	Brasilia	164,400,000	Real	Portuguese	8,511,970
	Argentina	Buenos Aires	35,000,000	Argentine peso	Spanish	2,766,890
	Peru	Lima	24,200,000	New sol	Spanish, Aymara, Quechua	1,285,220
	Colombia	Bogotá	35,700,000	Colombian peso	Spanish	1,138,910

FLAG	COUNTRY	CAPITAL	POPULATION	CURRENCY	OFFICIAL LANG.	AREA (SQ KM)
	Bolivia	La Paz	7,600,000	Boliviano	Spanish, Aymara, Quechua	1,098,580
	Venezuela	Caracas	22,300,000	Bolívar	Spanish	912,050
	Chile	Santiago	14,500,000	Chilean peso	Spanish	756,950
	Paraguay	Asunción	5,100,000	Guaraní	Spanish, Guaraní	406,750
	Ecuador	Quito	11,700,000	Sucre	Spanish	283, 56
	Guyana	Georgetown	800,000	Guyana dollar	English	214, 970
	Uruguay	Montevideo	3,200,000	Uruguayan peso	Spanish	177,410
	Surinam	Paramaribo	400,000	Surinam guilder	Dutch	163,270
	Nicaragua	Managua	4,600,000	New córdoba	Spanish	130,000
	Honduras	Tegucigalpa	5,800,000	Lempira	Spanish	112,090
	Cuba	Havana	11,100,000	Cuban peso	Spanish	110,860
	Guatemala	Guatemala City	10,900,000	Quetzal	Spanish	108,890
	Panama	Panama City	2,700,000	Balboa	Spanish	77,080
	Costa Rica	San José	3,500,000	Costa Rican dollar	Spanish	51,100
	Dominican Republic	Santo Domingo	8,000,000	Dominican Republic peso	Spanish	48,750
	Haiti	Port-au-Prince	7,300,000	Gourde	French, French Creole	27,750
	Belize	Belmopan	200,000	Belizean dollar	English	22,960
	El Salvador	San Salvador	5,900,000	Colón	Spanish	21,040
	Bahamas	Nassau	300,000	Bahamian dollar	English	13,800
	Jamaica	Kingston	2,500,000	Jamaican dollar	English	10,990
	Trinidad & Tobago	Port-of-Spain	1,300,000	Trinidad and Tobago dollar	English	5,130

FLAG	COUNTRY	CAPITAL	POPULATION	CURRENCY	OFFICIAL LANG.	AREA (SQ KM)
	Dominica	Roseau	71,000	East Caribbean dollar	English	750
	St Lucia	Castries	141,000	East Caribbean dollar	English	620
	Antigua & Barbuda	St John's	65,000	East Caribbean dollar	English	440
	Barbados	Bridgetown	300,000	Barbados dollar	English	430
	St Kitts & Nevis	Basseterre	41,000	East Caribbean dollar	English	360
	St Vincent & the Grenadines	Kingstown	111,000	East Caribbean dollar	English	340
	Grenada	St George's	92,000	East Caribbean dollar	English	340

			EUROPE			
FLAG	COUNTRY	CAPITAL	POPULATION	CURRENCY	OFFICIAL LANG.	AREA (SQ KM)
	Russian Federation	Moscow	146,700,000	Rouble	Russian	173,750,400
	Ukraine	Kiev	51,300,000	Karbovanets	Ukrainian	603,700
	France	Paris	58,200,000	Franc	French	551,500
	Spain	Madrid	39,700,000	Peseta	Spanish, Galician, Basque, Catalan	504,780
	Sweden	Stockholm	8,800,000	Swedish krona	Swedish	449,960
	Germany	Berlin	81,800,000	Deutsche Mark	German	356,910
	Finland	Helsinki	5,100,000	Markka	Finnish, Swedish	338,130
	Norway	Oslo	4,400,000	Norwegian krone	Norwegian	323,900
	Poland	Warsaw	38,400,000	Zloty	Polish	312,680
	Italy	Rome	57,200,000	Italian lira	Italian	301,270
	United Kingdom	London	58,400,000	Pound sterling	English	244,880
	Romania	Bucharest	22,800,000	Leu	Romanian	237,500
	Belorussia	Minsk	10,100,000	Belorussian rouble	Belorussian	207,600

FLAG	COUNTRY	CAPITAL	POPULATION	CURRENCY	OFFICIAL LANG.	AREA (SQ KM)
	Greece	Athens	10,500,000	Drachma	Greek	131,990
	Bulgaria	Sofia	8,700,000	Lev	Bulgarian	110,910
	Iceland	Reykjavík	300,000	New Icelandic króna	Icelandic	103,000
	Yugoslavia	Belgrade	10,900,000	Dinar	Serbo-Croatian	102,173
	Hungary	Budapest	10,100,000	Forint	Hungarian (Magyar)	93,030
	Portugal	Lisbon	9,800,000	Escudo	Portuguese	92,390
	Austria	Vienna	8,000,000	Austrian schilling	German	83,850
	Czech Republic	Prague	10,300,000	Czech koruna	Czech	78,370
	Ireland	Dublin	3,600,000	Irish pound	Irish, English	70,280
	Latvia	Riga	2,500,000	Lats	Latvian	64,589
	Lithuania	Vilnius	3,700,000	Litas	Lithuanian	65,200
	Croatia	Zagreb	4,500,000	Kuna	Croatian	56,540
	Bosnia & Herzegovina	Sarajevo	3,500,000	Bosnian dinar	Serbo-Croatian	51,130
	Slovakia	Bratislava	5,400,000	Slovak koruna	Slovak	49,500
	Estonia	Tallinn	1,500,000	Kroon	Estonian	42,125
	Denmark	Copenhagen	5,200,000	Danish kroner	Danish	43,070
	Switzerland	Bern	7,300,000	Swiss franc	German, French, Italian	41,290
	Netherlands	Amsterdam, The Hague	15,600,000	Netherlands guilder	Dutch	37,330
	Moldova	Chisinau	4,400,000	Moldovan leu	Romanian	33,700
	Belgium	Brussels	10,100,000	Belgian franc	Dutch, French, German	33,100
	Albania	Tirana	3,500,000	New lek	Albanian	28,750

FLAG	COUNTRY	CAPITAL	POPULATION	CURRENCY	OFFICIAL LANG.	AREA (SQ KM)
	Macedonia	Skopje	2,200,000	Macedonian denar	None	25,715
	Slovenia	Ljubljana	1,900,000	Tolar	Slovene	20,250
	Luxembourg	Luxembourg	400,000	Luxembourg franc	Letzeburgish	2,586
	Andorra	Andorra la Vella	65,000	French franc, Spanish peseta	Catalan	468
	Malta	Valletta	400,000	Maltese lira	Maltese, English	320
	Liechtenstein	Vaduz	31,000	Swiss franc	German	160
	San Marino	San Marino	25,000	Italian lira	Italian	61
	Monaco	Monaco	31,000	French franc	French	1.95
	Vatican City	Not applicable	1,000	Lira	Italian, Latin	0.44

ASIA

FLAG	COUNTRY	CAPITAL	POPULATION	CURRENCY	OFFICIAL LANG.	AREA (SQ KM)
	China	Beijing	1,234,300,000	Yuan	Mandarin	9,396,960
	India	New Delhi	953,000,000	Rupee	Hindi, English	3,287,590
	Kazakhstan	Alma-Ata	17,200,000	Tenge	Kazakh	2,717,300
	Saudi Arabia	Riyadh	18,400,000	Saudi riyal	Arabic	2,149,690
	Indonesia	Jakarta	200,600,000	Rupiah	Bahasa Indonesia	1,904,570
	Iran	Tehran	68,700,000	Iranian rial	Farsi	1,648,000
	Mongolia	Ulan Bator	2,500,000	Tughrik	Khalkh Mongol	1,565,000
	Pakistan	Islamabad	144,500,000	Pakistani rupee	Urdu	796,100
	Turkey	Ankara	63,100,000	Turkish lira	Turkish	779,450
	Burma (Myanmar)	Rangoon (Yangon)	47,500,000	Kyat	Burmese (Myanmar)	676,550
	Afghanistan	Kabul	21,500,000	Afghani	Persian, Pashtu	652,090

Flag	Country	Capital	Population	Currency	Official lang.	Area (sq km)
	Yemen	Sana	15,100,000	Yemen rial, Yemen dinar	Arabic	527,970
	Thailand	Bangkok	59,400,000	Baht	Thai	513,120
	Turkmenistan	Ashgabad	4,200,000	Manat	Turkmen	488,100
	Uzbekistan	Tashkent	23,300,000	Som	Uzbek	447,400
	Iraq	Baghdad	21,000,000	Iraqi dinar	Arabic	438,320
	Japan	Tokyo	125,400,000	Yen	Japanese	377,800
	Malaysia	Kuala Lumpur	20,600,000	Ringgit	Malay	329,750
	Vietnam	Hanoi	76,200,000	New dông	Vietnamese	329,560
	Philippines	Manila	69,000,000	Philippine peso	Filipino, English	300,000
	Laos	Vientiane	5,000,000	Kip	Lao	236,800
	Oman	Muscat	2,300,000	Omani rial	Arabic	212,460
	Kyrgyzstan	Bishkek	4,800,000	Som	Kyrgyz	198,500
	Syria	Damascus	15,200,000	Syrian pound	Arabic	185,180
	Cambodia	Phnom Penh	10,500,000	Riel	Khmer	181,040
	Bangladesh	Dhaka	123,100,000	Taka	Bengali	143,998
	Tajikistan	Dushanbe	6,300,000	Rouble	Tajik	143,100
	Nepal	Kathmandu	22,500,000	Nepalese rupee	Nepali	140,800
	North Korea	Pyongyang	24,300,000	Won	Korean	120,540
	South Korea	Seoul	45,400,000	Won	Korean	99,020
	Jordan	Amman	5,700,000	Jordanian dinar	Arabic	89,210
	Azerbaijan	Baku	7,600,000	Manat	Azerbaijani	86,600

FLAG	COUNTRY	CAPITAL	POPULATION	CURRENCY	OFFICIAL LANG.	AREA (SQ KM)
	United Arab Emirates	Abu Dhabi	1,900,000	UAE dirham	Arabic	83,600
	Georgia	Tbilisi	5,500,000	Coupon	Georgian	69,700
	Sri Lanka	Colombo	18,600,000	Sri Lanka rupee	Sinhalese	65,610
	Bhutan	Thimpu	1,700,000	Ngultrum	Dzongkha	47,000
	Taiwan	Taipei	21,125,792	New Taiwan dollar	Mandarin	36,179
	Armenia	Yerevan	3,600,000	Dram	Armenian	29,000
	Israel	Jerusalem	5,800,000	New shekel	Hebrew	20,700
	Kuwait	Kuwait City	1,500,000	Kuwaiti dinar	Arabic	17,820
	Qatar	Doha	600,000	Qatar riyal	Arabic	11,000
	Lebanon	Beirut	3,100,000	Lebanese pound	Arabic	10,400
	Cyprus	Nicosia	800,000	Cyprus pound (Turkish lira)	Greek (Turkish)	9,251
	Brunei	Bandar Seri Begawan	300,000	Brunei dollar	Malay	5,770
	Bahrain	Manama	600,000	Bahrain dinar	Arabic	680
	Singapore	Singapore City	2,900,000	Singapore dollar	Malay, Chinese, Tamil, English	620
	Maldives	Male	300,000	Rufiyaa	Dhivehi	300
AFRICA						
FLAG	COUNTRY	CAPITAL	POPULATION	CURRENCY	OFFICIAL LANG.	AREA (SQ KM)
	Sudan	Khartoum	28,900,000	Sudanese dinar	Arabic	2,505,810
	Algeria	Algiers	28,600,000	Algerian dinar	Arabic	2,381,740
	Congo (Zaire)	Kinshasa	45,300,000	New zaire	French	2,345,410
	Libya	Tripoli	5,600,000	Libyan dinar	Arabic	1,759,540
	Chad	N'Djamena	6,500,000	CFA franc	French	1,284,000

FLAG	COUNTRY	CAPITAL	POPULATION	CURRENCY	OFFICIAL LANG.	AREA (SQ KM)
	Niger	Niamey	9,500,000	CFA franc	French	1,267,000
	Angola	Luanda	11,500,000	New kwanza	Portuguese	1,246,700
	Mali	Bamako	11,100,000	CFA franc	French	1,240,190
	Ethiopia	Addis Ababa	56,700,000	Ethiopian birr	Amharic	1,221,900
	South Africa	Pretoria, Cape Town, Bloemfontein	42,400,000	Rand	11 African languages, English, Afrikaans	1,221,040
	Mauritania	Nouakchott	2,300,000	Ouguiya	French	1,025,520
	Egypt	Cairo	64,200,000	Egyptian pound	Arabic	1,001,450
	Tanzania	Dodoma	30,500,000	Tanzanian shilling	English, Swahili	945,090
	Nigeria	Abuja	115,000,000	Naira	English	923,770
	Namibia	Windhoek	1,600,000	South African rand	English	824,290
	Mozambique	Maputo	16,500,000	Metical	Portuguese	801,590
	Zambia	Lusaka	9,700,000	Zambian kwacha	English, Bemba, Nyanja	752,610
	Somalia	Mogadishu	9,500,000	Somali shilling	Somali, Arabic	637,660
	Central African Republic	Bangui	3,400,000	CFA franc	French	622,980
	Madagascar	Antananarivo	15,200,000	Malagasy franc	Malagasy, French	587,040
	Botswana	Gaborone	1,500,000	Pula	English	581,730
	Kenya	Nairobi	29,100,000	Kenya shilling	Swahili	580,370
	Cameroon	Yaoundé	13,600,000	CFA franc	French, English	475,440
	Morocco (+W. Sahara)	Rabat	27,600,000	Moroccan dirham	Arabic	446,550 (+156,650)
	Zimbabwe	Harare	11,500,000	Zimbabwe dollar	English	390,580
	Congo	Brazzaville	2,700,000	CFA franc	French	342,000

FLAG	COUNTRY	CAPITAL	POPULATION	CURRENCY	OFFICIAL LANG.	AREA (SQ KM)
	Ivory Coast	Yamoussoukro	14,700,000	CFA franc	French	322,463
	Burkina	Ouagadougou	10,600,000	CFA franc	French	274,200
	Gabon	Libreville	1,400,000	CFA franc	French	267,670
	Guinea	Conakry	6,900,000	Guinea franc	French	245,860
	Ghana	Accra	18,000,000	Cedi	English	238,540
	Uganda	Kampala	22,000,000	New Uganda shilling	English	235,880
	Senegal	Dakar	8,500,000	CFA franc	French	196,720
	Tunisia	Tunis	9,100,000	Tunisian dinar	Arabic	163,610
	Malawi	Lilongwe	11,400,000	Malawian kwacha	Chewa, English	118,480
	Benin	Porto-Novo	5,600,000	CFA franc	French	112,620
	Liberia	Monrovia	3,100,000	Liberian dollar	English	111,370
	Eritrea	Asmara	3,600,000	Egyptian pound	Tigrinya, Arabic	93,680
	Sierra Leone	Freetown	4,600,000	Leone	English	71,740
	Togo	Lomé	4,300,000	CFA franc	French, Kabye, Ewe	56,790
	Guinea-Bissau	Bissau	1,100,000	Guinea peso	Portuguese	36,120
	Lesotho	Maseru	2,100,000	Loti	English, Sesotho	30,350
	Equatorial Guinea	Malabo	400,000	CFA franc	Spanish	28,050
	Burundi	Bujumbura	6,600,000	Burundi franc	French, Kirundi	27,830
	Rwanda	Kigali	8,200,000	Rwanda franc	French, Kinyarwanda	26,340
	Djibouti	Djibouti	600,000	Djibouti franc	Arabic, French	23,200
	Swaziland	Mbabane	900,000	Lilangeni	Siswati, English	17,360

FLAG	COUNTRY	CAPITAL	POPULATION	CURRENCY	OFFICIAL LANG.	AREA (SQ KM)
	Gambia	Banjul	1,200,000	Dalasi	English	11,300
	Cape Verde	Cidade de Praia	400,000	Cape Verde escudo	Portuguese	4,030
	Comoros	Moroni	700,000	Comoros franc	Arabic, French	2,230
	Mauritius	Port Louis	1,100,000	Mauritian rupee	English	1860
	São Tomé & Principe	São Tomé	125,000	Dobra	Portuguese	964
	Seychelles	Victoria	74,000	Seychelles rupee	Creole	280
AUSTRALASIA AND OCEANIA						
FLAG	COUNTRY	CAPITAL	POPULATION	CURRENCY	OFFICIAL LANG.	AREA (SQ KM)
	Australia	Canberra	18,300,000	Australian dollar	English	7,686,850
	Papua New Guinea	Port Moresby	4,400,000	Kina	Pidgin English, Motu	462,840
	New Zealand	Wellington	3,600,000	New Zealand dollar	English	268,680
	Solomon Islands	Honiara	400,000	Solomon Islands dollar	English	289,000
	Fiji	Suva	800,000	Fiji dollar	English	18,270
	Vanuatu	Port-Vila	200,000	Vatu	English, French	12,190
	Micronesia	Kolonia	104,000	US dollar	English	2,900
	Western Samoa	Apia	200,000	Tala	Samoan, English	2,840
	Tonga	Nuku'alofa	98,000	Pa'anga	Tongan	750
	Kiribati	Bairiki	77,000	Australian dollar	English	710
	Palau	Koror	16,500	US dollar	Palauan, English	460
	Marshall Islands	Majuro	54,000	US dollar	English, Marshallese	181
	Tuvalu	Funafuti	9,000	Australian dollar, Tuvaluan dollar	None	26
	Nauru	None	11,000	Australian dollar	Nauruan	21

AMERICAN STATES

THE UNITED STATES OF AMERICA is made up of 50 states and the District of Columbia (also known as Washington, D.C.). The two most recently enlisted states, Alaska and Hawaii (both 1959), are separate from the main landmass.

ALASKA
0   500 km
0   500 miles

ALASKA JUNEAU •

ALASKA
Alaska, the largest in area, is the least populated state. In 1867, the US bought Alaska from Russia for only $7.2 million. Today, great deposits of oil and natural gas, found in 1968, are mined.

HAWAII
0   200 km
0   200 miles

HAWAII
Consisting of a group of about 130 Pacific islands, Hawaii is 3,365 km from the continental US. It is the most recent state of the US, and is best known for its volcanic activity.

Olympia •
WASHINGTON
Salem •   • Helena
OREGON   MONTA

• Boise
IDAHO
W
NEVADA
Cheye
Sacramento   • Carson City Salt Lake City
•   UTAH
CALIFORNIA   CO

ARIZONA
Los Angeles •   Santa
NEW
Phoenix   MEXIC

M   E   X   I   C   O

THE WHITE HOUSE
The White House in
Washington, DC, is the
official residence of the
President and his family.
Designed by James
Hoban, it was destroyed
by British troops in 1814
and then rebuilt.

UNITED STATES

0   400 km

0   400 miles

CANADA

NORTH DAKOTA
• Bismark

MINNESOTA

MAINE
• Augusta

VERM.
Montpelier NEW HAM.

St Paul •

WISCONSIN

NEW YORK Concord •

SOUTH DAKOTA
• Pierre

Albany • MASS. • Boston
Providence •
Hartford • RHODE IS.
CONN.

NG

Madison •

MICHIGAN
Lansing •

I O W A

INDIANA OHIO

PENNSYLVANIA NEW JERSEY
Harrisburg • • Trenton

NEBRASKA
Lincoln •

Des Moines •

MARYLAND
DELAWARE

Denver

Springfield •

Columbus • WEST
VIRGINIA
Charleston •

Topeka •

ILLINOIS

Indianapolis •

DO

KANSAS

• Jefferson
City

Frankfort •

VIRGINIA
• Richmond

MISSOURI

KENTUCKY

NORTH
• Raleigh

Oklahoma
City •

• Nashville

CAROLINA

OKLAHOMA

ARKANSAS TENNESSEE

Columbia
•

TEXAS

Little Rock •

ALABAMA Atlanta
•

SOUTH
CAROLINA

MISSISSIPPI

GEORGIA

N

Jackson • Montgomery •

LOUISIANA

• Tallahassee

• Austin

Baton
Rouge •

FLORIDA

COAL

WORLD RESOURCES

THE BASIC RAW MATERIALS for living all come from the Earth. Some are renewable resources, like cultivated foods, while others, such as fossil fuels, are non-renewable. As the global population increases, so humankind draws relentlessly on the Earth. This has led to wasteful exploitation of resources in order to satisfy modern "needs".

COAL

The table shows the world's top producers per annum.

COUNTRY	TONNES
China	1,116,369,000
US	904,959,000
Germany	458,102,000
Russia	313,960,000
India	254,600,000

CRUDE OIL

The table shows production in barrels per annum.

COUNTRY	BARRELS P.A.
Saudi Arabia	2,979,000,000
Russia	65,374,000
US	56,762,000
Iran	42,480,000
China	29,324,000

ELECTRICITY

The table shows production annually in kilo-watt hours.

COUNTRY	KW/HR
US	3,074,504,000,000
Russia	904,959,000
Japan	458,102,000
China	313,960,000
Germany	254,600,000

LEADING PRODUCERS OF MINERALS

MATERIAL	TOP PRODUCERS	TOTAL* (in millions)	WORLD TOTAL* (in millions)
Bauxite	Australia	37.4	
	Guinea	16.5	1,064
Coal	China	1,054	
	US	889	5,882
Copper	Chile	1.6	
	US	1.5	9.2
Natural gas	Russia	0.80 m³	
	US	0.49 m³	2.1 m³
Iron ore	Russia	241	
	China	165	984
Kaolin (clay)	Russia	2.0	
	South Korea	1.3	23.1
Salt	US	35.5	
	China	28.3	
Sulphur	US	11.6	
	China	7.4	60.3

*All figures in tonnes apart from m³ = cubic metres.

WHEAT	
These tables show the top producers of staple crops.	
COUNTRY	TONNES
China	105,005,000
US	65,374,000
India	56,762,000
Russia	42,480,000
France	29,324,000
Canada	27,825,000

RICE	
Rice is the only crop that can support Asia's population.	
COUNTRY	TONNES
China	187,211,000
India	111,011,000
Indonesia	47,883,000
Bangladesh	28,000,000
Vietnam	22,300,000
Thailand	19,090,000

MAIZE	
First grown in the Americas, maize is a prime cereal crop.	
COUNTRY	TONNES
US	161,145,000
China	103,380,000
Brazil	29,967,000
Mexico	18,600,000
France	14,966,000
Argentina	10,897,000

LEADING AGRICULTURAL PRODUCERS

Today, farming and fishing are major international businesses, with countries competing in the export market. This table shows where products are derived by listing the top three producers of wide-ranging agricultural products.

PRODUCT	TOP PRODUCER	SECOND	THIRD
Cattle	Australia	Brazil	US
Coffee	Brazil	Colombia	Indonesia
Cotton	China	US	Russia
Cow's milk	US	Germany	Russia
Hen's eggs	China	US	Russia
Hogs	China	US	Russia
Maize	US	China	Brazil
Oats	Russia	US	Canada
Potatoes	Russia	Poland	China
Rice	China	India	Indonesia
Rubber	Malaysia	Indonesia	Thailand
Sheep	Australia	China	New Zealand
Soy beans	US	Brazil	China
Tea	India	China	Sri Lanka
Tobacco	China	US	India
Wheat	China	US	India
Wood	US	Russia	China
Wool	Australia	Russia	New Zealand

FISH CATCHES

This table gives fish catches per year in the given area.

AREA	TONNES*
Pacific Ocean	48.32
Atlantic Ocean	20.17
Indian Ocean	5.93
Mediterranean and Black Sea	1.29
Antarctic	0.40
World total	76.11

*catch in million metric tonnes (1989–91)

FISHING IN THE NORTH SEA

LINCOLN MEMORIAL, WASHINGTON, DC.

US PRESIDENTS

WITH THE END of the Cold War in the 1990s, the President of the US became the most powerful leader in the world. Presidents are elected to serve a 4-year term of office. Since 1951, no president is permitted to serve more than two terms.

PRESIDENTS OF THE US			
1789–97	George Washington	1885–89	Grover S. Cleveland
1797–1801	John Adams	1889–93	Benjamin Harrison
1801–09	Thomas Jefferson	1893–97	Grover S. Cleveland
1809–17	James Madison	1897–1901	William McKinley
1817–25	James Monroe	1901–09	Theodore Roosevelt
1825–29	John Quincy Adams	1909–13	William H. Taft
1829–37	Andrew Jackson	1913–21	Woodrow Wilson
1837–41	Martin van Buren	1921–23	Warren G. Harding
1841	William H. Harrison	1923–29	Calvin Coolidge
1841–45	John Tyler	1929–33	Herbert Hoover
1845–49	James K. Polk	1933–45	Franklin D. Roosevelt
1849–50	Zachary Taylor	1945–53	Harry S. Truman
1850–53	Millard Fillmore	1953–61	Dwight D. Eisenhower
1853–57	Franklin Pierce	1961–63	John F. Kennedy
1857–61	James Buchanan	1963–69	Lyndon B. Johnson
1861–65	Abraham Lincoln	1969–74	Richard Nixon
1865–69	Andrew Johnson	1974–77	Gerald Ford
1869–77	Ulysses S. Grant	1977–81	James Carter
1877–81	Rutherford B. Hayes	1981–89	Ronald Reagan
1881	James A. Garfield	1989–93	George Bush
1881–85	Chester A. Arthur	1993–	William J. Clinton

RUSSIAN RULERS

FOR MOST OF ITS HISTORY, Russia was a monarchy in which the Tsar or Tsarina held absolute power. The 1917 Bolshevik Revolution changed the style of politics, as did the fall of Communism in 1992. Today, supreme power lies with an elected president.

RUSSIAN MONARCHS			
1462–1505	Ivan III, the Great	1725–27	Catherine I
1505–33	Basil III	1727–30	Peter II
1533–84	Ivan IV, the Terrible	1730–40	Anna
1584–98	Fyodor I	1740–41	Ivan VI
1598–1605	Boris Gudunov	1741–62	Elizabeth
1605	Fyodor II	1762	Peter III
1605–06	Demetrius	1762–96	Catherine II, the Great
1606–10	Basil (IV) Shuiski	1796–1801	Paul I
1610–13	Interregnum (interval in reigns)	1801–25	Alexander I
1613–45	Michael Romanov	1825–55	Nicholas I
1645–76	Alexis	1855–81	Alexander II
1676–82	Fyodor III	1881–94	Alexander III
1682–89	Ivan V and Peter I, the Great	1894–1917	Nicholas II
1689–1725	Peter I, the Great	1917	Bolshevik Revolution

RUSSIAN LEADERS

JOSEPH STALIN

1917–22	Vladimir Lenin
1922–53	Joseph Stalin
1953–64	Nikita Krushchev
1964–82	Leonid Brezhnev
1982–84	Yuri Andropov
1984–85	Konstantin Chernenko
1985–92	Mikhail Gorbachev
1992–	Boris Yeltsin

SPASSKY TOWER
This is the most impressive tower in the Kremlin, Moscow's ruling centre.

British rulers

These lists detail the monarchs of England and Scotland up to the early 17th century and, following the unification of England and Scotland, the joint British monarchs up to the present day.

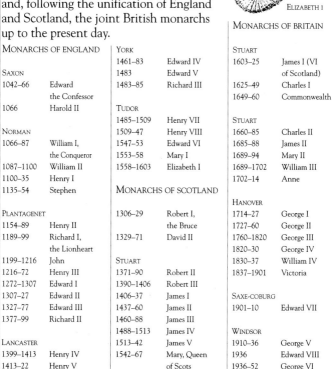

ELIZABETH I

MONARCHS OF ENGLAND

SAXON

1042–66	Edward the Confessor
1066	Harold II

NORMAN

1066–87	William I, the Conqueror
1087–1100	William II
1100–35	Henry I
1135–54	Stephen

PLANTAGENET

1154–89	Henry II
1189–99	Richard I, the Lionheart
1199–1216	John
1216–72	Henry III
1272–1307	Edward I
1307–27	Edward II
1327–77	Edward III
1377–99	Richard II

LANCASTER

1399–1413	Henry IV
1413–22	Henry V
1422–61	Henry VI

YORK

1461–83	Edward IV
1483	Edward V
1483–85	Richard III

TUDOR

1485–1509	Henry VII
1509–47	Henry VIII
1547–53	Edward VI
1553–58	Mary I
1558–1603	Elizabeth I

MONARCHS OF SCOTLAND

1306–29	Robert I, the Bruce
1329–71	David II

STUART

1371–90	Robert II
1390–1406	Robert III
1406–37	James I
1437–60	James II
1460–88	James III
1488–1513	James IV
1513–42	James V
1542–67	Mary, Queen of Scots
1567–1625	James VI

MONARCHS OF BRITAIN

STUART

1603–25	James I (VI of Scotland)
1625–49	Charles I
1649–60	Commonwealth

STUART

1660–85	Charles II
1685–88	James II
1689–94	Mary II
1689–1702	William III
1702–14	Anne

HANOVER

1714–27	George I
1727–60	George II
1760–1820	George III
1820–30	George IV
1830–37	William IV
1837–1901	Victoria

SAXE-COBURG

1901–10	Edward VII

WINDSOR

1910–36	George V
1936	Edward VIII
1936–52	George VI
1952–	Elizabeth II

BRITISH PRIME MINISTERS

1721–42	Robert Walpole	1859–65	Viscount Palmerston
1742–43	Earl of Wilmington	1865–66	Earl Russell
1743–54	Henry Pelham	1866–68	Earl of Derby
1754–56	Duke of Newcastle	1868	Benjamin Disraeli
1756–57	Duke of Devonshire	1868–74	William Gladstone
1757–62	Duke of Newcastle	1874–80	Benjamin Disraeli
1762–63	Earl of Bute	1880–85	William Gladstone
1763–65	George Grenville	1885–86	Marquess of Salisbury
1765–66	Marquess of Rockingham	1886	William Gladstone
1766–68	Earl of Chatham,	1886–92	Marquess of Salisbury
	Pitt the Elder	1892–94	William Gladstone
1768–70	Duke of Grafton	1894–95	Earl of Rosebery
1770–82	Lord North	1895–1902	Marquess of Salisbury
1782	Marquess of Rockingham	1902–05	Arthur Balfour
1782–83	Earl of Shelburne	1905–08	Henry Campbell-Bannerman
1783	Duke of Portland	1908–16	Herbert Asquith
1783–1801	William Pitt, the Younger	1916–22	David Lloyd George
1801–04	Henry Addington	1922–23	Andrew Bonar Law
1804–06	William Pitt, the Younger	1923–24	Stanley Baldwin
1806–07	Lord Grenville	1924	James Ramsay MacDonald
1807–09	Duke of Portland	1924–29	Stanley Baldwin
1809–12	Spencer Perceval	1929–35	James Ramsay MacDonald
1812–27	Earl of Liverpool	1935–37	Stanley Baldwin
1827	George Canning	1937–40	Neville Chamberlain
1827–28	Viscount Goderich	1940–45	Winston Churchill
1828–30	Duke of Wellington	1945–51	Clement Attlee
1830–34	Earl Grey	1951–55	Winston Churchill
1834	Viscount Melbourne	1955–57	Anthony Eden
1834–35	Robert Peel	1957–63	Harold Macmillan
1835–41	Viscount Melbourne	1963–64	Sir Alec Douglas-Home
1841–46	Robert Peel	1964–70	Harold Wilson
1846–52	Lord John Russell	1970–74	Edward Heath
1852	Earl of Derby	1974–76	Harold Wilson
1852–55	Earl of Aberdeen	1976–79	James Callaghan
1855–58	Viscount Palmerston	1979–90	Margaret Thatcher
1858–59	Earl of Derby	1990–97	John Major
		1997–	Tony Blair

Ancient rulers and dynasties

Throughout history, many civilizations have endured over long periods of time. The ancient Egyptians established an extremely advanced society, consolidating ruling power around the cult of the pharaoh. The Chinese passed on their culture in the form of succeeding dynasties. The Japanese characterized their history through succeeding periods that coloured political, military, and cultural life. The Catholic Church has maintained its inheritance through a lineage of popes that extends directly from St Peter.

OSIRIS, EGYPTIAN GOD OF THE UNDERWORLD

EGYPTIAN PERIODS		
PERIOD	DATE	MAIN PHARAOH
Early dynastic	c.3100–c.2686 BC	Narmer (Menes)
Old Kingdom	c.2686–c.2160 BC	Zoser
		Khufu
First Intermediate Period	c.2160–c.2130 BC	
Middle Kingdom	c.2130–c.1786 BC	Mentuhotep II
Second Intermediate Period	c.1786–c.1550 BC	Hyksos rule
New Kingdom	c.1550–c.1050 BC	Amenhotep I
		Queen Hatshepsut
		Thutmose III
		Akhenaton
		Tutankhamun
		Rameses II
Third Intermediate Period	c.1050–667 BC	Nubian rule
Early dynastic	c.664–333 BC	Darius III
Early dynastic	333–30 BC	Alexander the Great
		Ptolemy I Soter
		Queen Cleopatra VII

KEY ROMAN RULERS

ROMAN REPUBLIC (RULERS)	REIGN
Lucius Cornelius Sulla	82–78 BC
Pompey, Crassus, Caesar	
(First Triumvirate)	60–53 BC
Pompey	52–47 BC
Julius Caesar	46–44 BC
Mark Antony, Octavian,	
Lepidus (Second Triumvirate)	43–31 BC
ROMAN EMPIRE (EMPERORS)	REIGN
Augustus (Octavian)	27 BC–AD 14
Tiberius	14–37
Caligula	37–41
Claudius	41–54
Nero	54–68
Vespasian	69–79
Titus	79–81
Domitian	81–96
Trajan	98–117

CHINESE DYNASTIES AND REPUBLICS

DYNASTY	DATES
Shang	1650–1027 BC
Zhou	1027–256 BC
Warring States	481–221 BC
Qin (Chin)	221–207 BC
Han	207 BC–AD 220
Period of Disunity	221–589
Sui	589–618
Tang	618–906
Five Dynasties	907–960
Song (Sung)	960–1279
Yuan (Mongol)	1279–1368
Ming	1368–1644
Qing (Manchu)	1644–1911
Republic (Nationalist)	1911–1949
People's Republic (Communist)	1949–

JAPANESE PERIODS*

PERIOD	DATE (AD)
Yamato	250–710
Nara	710–794
Heian	794–1192
Kamakura	1192–1333
Muromachi	1333–1573
Momoyama	1573–1603
Edo	1603–1867
Meiji	1867–1912
Taisho	1912–1926
Showa	1926–1989
Heisei	1989–

JAPANESE WARLORD

*Japanese historical periods began with political unity and the introduction of an emperor figure.

KEY POPES

POPE	REIGN (AD)
St Peter	c.42–67
St Clement I	c.88–97
St Stephen I	254–257
St Leo I, the Great	440–461
St Gregory I, the Great	590–604
St Leo IX	1049–54
St Gregory VII	1073–85
Urban II	1088–99
Innocent III	1198–1216
Alexander VI	1492–1503
Paul III	1534–49
Gregory XIII	1572–85
Pius IX	1846–78
John XXIII	1958–63
John Paul II	1978–

ROSARY BEADS

MAJOR WARS

IN THE PAST, wars were decided by armies on battlefields. Today, technology has vastly increased modern warfare's destructive power.

GATLING GUN

MAJOR WARS AND REVOLUTIONS			
DATE	CONFLICT	VICTOR(S)	LOSER(S)
c.1096–1291	Crusades	Muslims	European Christians
c.1337–1453	Hundred Years War	France	England
1455–85	Wars of the Roses	House of Lancaster	House of York
1618–48	Thirty Years War	European Protestants	European Catholics
1642–49	English Civil War	Parliamentarians	Royalists
1701–13	War of the Spanish Succession	Austria	France
1756–63	Seven Years War	Britain, Hanover, Prussia	Austria, France, Russia, Sweden
1775–83	American Revolution	American colonies	Britain
1789	French Revolution	Jacobins	Royalists
1792–1815	Napoleonic Wars	Austria, Britain, Russia, Prussia, Sweden	France
1812–14	War of 1812	US	Britain
1846–48	Mexican–American War	US	Mexico
1853–56	Crimean War	Britain, France, Sardinia, Turkey	Russia
1861–65	American Civil War	Unionists	Confederates
1870–71	Franco–Prussian War	Prussia	France
1899–1902	Second Boer War	British Commonwealth	Boers
1904–05	Russo–Japanese War	Japan	Russia

GERMAN SWEPT-HILT RAPIER

DATE	CONFLICT	VICTOR(S)	LOSER(S)
1917	Russian Revolution	Bolsheviks	Royalists
1914–18	World War I	British Commonwealth, Belgium, France, Italy, Russia, US	Germany, Austria-Hungary, Turkey
1936–39	Spanish Civil War	Nationalists	Republicans
1937–45	Chinese–Japanese War	China	Japan
1939–45	World War II	British Commonwealth, USSR, US	Germany, Italy, Japan
1945–49	Chinese Revolution	Communists	Nationalists
1950–53	Korean War	South Korea, UN	North Korea
1965–75	Vietnam War	North Vietnam	South Vietnam, US and allies
1967	Six-Day War	Israel	Egypt
1967–70	Nigerian Civil War	Federalists	Biafrans
1973	October War	Israel	Arab nations
1980–88	Iran–Iraq War	negotiated ceasefire	
1991	Gulf War	US-led coalition	Iraq
1992–95	Bosnian Civil War	negotiated ceasefire	

NAZI STANDARD BEARER

KEY BATTLES			
DATE	NAME	VICTOR(S)	LOSER(S)
1066	Hastings (England)	Normans	Saxons
1415	Agincourt (France)	England	France
1588	Spanish Armada (England)	England	Spain
1805	Trafalgar	Britain	France, Spain
1805	Austerlitz (Czech Republic)	France	Austria, Russia
1815	Waterloo (Belgium)	Britain, Holland, Belgium, Prussia	France
1863	Gettysburg (US)	Unionists	Confederates
1916	The Somme (France)	British Commonwealth	Germany
1942	Midway (Pacific)	US	Japan
1943	Stalingrad (Russia)	USSR	Germany
1944	Normandy (France)	US, British Commonwealth	Germany

WAR FACTS

• War this century has killed 100 million people; 20 million since 1945.

• In World War I, about 19 million died: 41% soldiers, 59% civilians.

• In World War II, more than 50 million died: 50% soldiers, 50% civilians.

• Over 150 wars have broken out since 1945.

TECHNOLOGY

TRANSPORT MILESTONES 62
ROAD AND RAIL 64
SEA AND AIR 66
COMMUNICATIONS 68
ENGINEERING 70
THE ELECTRONIC BRAIN 72

TRANSPORT MILESTONES

THROUGHOUT HISTORY, people have always desired to move as quickly and freely as possible. Human ingenuity has led to countless transport inventions, from the invention of the wheel to the jet engine.

8000 BC – AD 1119	1522 – 1815	1829 – 1881
•8000 BC First long-distance sea voyage, from the Greek mainland to the island of Melos. •4500 BC Europe, Turkey, Iran: horses tamed for the first time. •3500 BC Wheeled vehicles in use in Mesopotamia.	•1522 Portuguese Ferdinand Magellan, in his ship the *Vittoria*, is the first person to sail around the world. •c.1700 Introduction of ship's steering wheel. •1776 A one-person submarine, The *Turtle*, designed by American David C. Bushnell is used in an attack on a British warship. •1783 French brothers Joseph and Étienne Montgolfier launch a hot-air balloon from Versailles, France. •1804 First successful steam locomotive built, by Englishman Richard Trevithick. •1815 Scotsman John L. McAdam develops macadam road-making material.	•1829 The *Rocket*, built by Englishman George Stephenson, ushers in the age of rail travel. •1830 UK: first public steam railway, called the Liverpool & Manchester. •1835 Invention of the screw propeller. •1839 Invention of the pedal-driven bicycle. •1852 Frenchman Henri Giffard builds and flies the first airship. •1869 Opening of the Suez Canal in Egypt. •1881 The world's first electric railway opens in Germany.

875–985
VIKING
LONGSHIP

•1900 BC First long-distance roads in Europe.
•605 Work completed on China's Grand Canal, which runs over 1000 km (600 miles).
•875–985 Viking ships dominate north European seas.
•1119 Early form of compass used by Chinese as navigation aid.

c.1700
SHIP'S WHEEL

1852
GIFFARD'S
AIRSHIP

1886 – 1913	1914 – 1955	1961 – 1999

1886 – 1913

- 1886 Gottlieb Daimler makes prototype car by fixing an engine to a horse-drawn carriage.
- 1890 UK: Opening of the first underground railway, the City and South London line.
- 1892 First commercially produced motorbike.
- 1892 German Rudolph Diesel develops the diesel engine.
- 1895 Germany's Kiel ship canal is completed.
- 1903 American Orville Wright makes the

1913
MODEL T FORD

first successful flight in the *Flyer*.
- 1907 Frenchman Paul Cornu makes the first helicopter flight.
- 1909 Frenchman Louis Blériot is first to fly the English Channel.
- 1910 American Henry Ford's Model T is the first mass-produced car.

1914 – 1955

- 1914 Panama Canal opens.

1939 HEINKEL HE 178

- 1919 First non-stop flight across the Atlantic by British aviators John Alcock and Arthur Whitten-Brown.
- 1926 Launch of the first liquid-fuelled rocket, designed by American Robert Goddard.
- 1937 British engineer Frank Whittle designs the jet engine.
- 1938 UK: The *Mallard* sets a world speed record for steam traction of 203 km/h (126 mph).
- 1939 The German Heinkel HE 178 makes the first jet-propelled flight.
- 1947 American test pilot Chuck Yeager breaks the sound barrier in a rocket-powered plane, the *Bell X-1*.
- 1952 The world's first jet airliner, the De Havilland Comet, enters service.
- 1955 US: Launch of the first nuclear submarine, the *Nautilus*.

1990 TGV TRAIN

1961 – 1999

- 1961 Russian Yuri Gagarin is the first person in space, in *Vostok I*.
- 1969 American astronauts Neil Armstrong and "Buzz" Aldrin land on the Moon, in *Apollo II*.
- 1970 The Boeing 747 "Jumbo Jet" comes into commercial service.
- 1981 A reusable spacecraft, US shuttle *Colombia*, is launched.
- 1986 The *Rutan Voyager* makes the first non-stop, round-the-world flight.
- 1990 France: a TGV electric train sets a world rail speed record of 515 km/h (320 mph).
- 1994 Opening of the Channel Tunnel rail link between France and England.
- 1997 British pilot Andy Green breaks the sound barrier on land in his jet car Thrust SSC.

ROAD AND RAIL

THE MOTOR VEHICLE AND TRAIN are the main forms of land transport. This century has witnessed ever-increasing road and rail networks that try to service burgeoning populations and economic growth. Pollution from motor transport is now a serious threat to the environment.

ROAD HAULAGE

Most goods are carried by motor transport since road networks can carry more traffic than railways. This table lists those countries that transport the most goods a year by road.

COUNTRY	GOODS TRANSPORTED (TONNES)
US	1,190,000,000
China	340,000,000
Russia	300,000,000
Japan	280,000,000
Brazil	270,000,000
India	220,000,000

COUNTRIES WITH THE MOST ROADS

COUNTRY	KM (MILES)
US	6,243,103 (3,879,284)
India	1,970,000 (1,224,101)
Brazil	1,670,148 (1,037,782)
Japan	1,510,750 (938,736)
China	1,115,609 (693,207)

TOP VEHICLE-OWNING COUNTRIES IN THE WORLD

COUNTRY	CARS	COMMERCIAL VEHICLES	TOTAL
US	134,981,000	65,465,000	200,446,000
Japan	44,680,000	22,173,463	66,853,463
Germany	40,499,442	3,061,874	43,561,316
Italy	30,000,000	2,806,500	32,806,500
France	25,100,000	5,195,000	30,295,000

TOP VEHICLE-PRODUCING COUNTRIES

COUNTRY	CARS	COMMERCIAL VEHICLES	TOTAL
US	6,083,227	5,715,678	11,798,905
Japan	7,863,763	2,482,023	10,345,786
Germany	4,539,583	303,326	4,842,909
France	3,147,622	442,965	3,590,587
South Korea	2,264,709	548,005	2,812,714

TRAFFIC JAMS
On average, car drivers spend 5.4 days per year in traffic jams.

EUROSTAR
Following the construction of the Channel Tunnel, a new train was specially designed to be used on this network. Known as "Eurostar", it can travel at a maximum speed of 300 km/h (186 mph).

LONGEST UNDERGROUND NETWORKS

CITY	STATIONS	KM (MILES)
Washington DC	86	612 (380)
London	272	430 (267)
New York	461	370 (230)
Paris (Metro & RER)	430	301 (187)
Moscow	115	225 (140)

RAILS
Rail lines are laid as a pair of continuous and parallel steel tracks, along which trains can run smoothly.

Switches allow trains to change direction

Wooden sleepers support steel tracks

LONGEST RAILROAD TUNNELS

TUNNEL	COUNTRY	DATE BUILT	LENGTH KM (MILES)
Seikan	Japan	1985	53.9 (33.5)
Channel	France/UK	1994	51.8 (32.2)
Mosco Metro	Russia	1979	30.7 (19.1)
Northern line	UK	1939	27.8 (17.3)
Daishimizu	Japan	1982	22.2 (13.8)

COUNTRES WITH THE MOST TRACK

COUNTRY	TOTAL KM (MILES) OF TRACK
US	240,000 (149,129)
Russia	158,100 (98,239)
Canada	146,444 (90,996)
China	64,000 (39,768)
India	61,850 (38,432)
Germany	45,468 (28,253)
Australia	40,478 (25,152)
France	34,322 (21,327)
Argentina	34,172 (21,223)
Brazil	30,133 (18,724)

TILTING TRAIN
The Italian ETR 450 tilts at an angle of up to 10°.

TRANSPORT FACTS
• At 4,787 m, Condor, Bolivia is the world's highest railway station.

• More than 130,000 steam locomotives were built in Britain from 1804–1968.

• General Motors in the US produces over 5.5 million cars a year.

SEA AND AIR

AS TECHNOLOGY increases communication around the world, so the ability to travel becomes more widespread. Today, shipping transports about 90% of international goods, aided by ship canals that provide shorter global routes. Airlines offer faster passenger services to world-wide destinations and carry millions of people every day.

HEATHROW AIRPORT
The busiest international airport in the world caters for over 40 million people each year. Business benefits the most from increased air travel, and many use Heathrow as a meeting point on connecting flights.

BUSIEST INTERNATIONAL AIRPORTS IN THE WORLD	
AIRPORT	INTERNATIONAL PASSENGERS PER ANNUM
London Heathrow, UK	44,262,000
Frankfurt, Germany	27,564,000
Charles de Gaulle, France	25,690,000
Hong Kong, China	25,248,000
Schipol, Netherlands	22,943,000
Tokyo/Narita, Japan	20,681,000
Singapore International	20,203,000
London Gatwick, UK	19,417,000
JFK International, US	15,898,000
Bangkok, Thailand	13,747,000

AIRLINE PASSENGER TRAFFIC 94–95	
AIRLINE	PASSENGERS (MILLIONS)
Alitalia Italian Airlines	20.0
American Airlines	80.0
British Airways	30.0
Delta Airlines	87.0
Emirates Airways	3.0
Gulf Air	5.0
JAL (Japan Air)	32.7
KLM (Royal Dutch Air)	11.2
Lufthansa (German Airlines)	40.7
Singapore Air	10.7
Virgin Atlantic Airways	2.0

MAJOR PORTS	
PORT (COUNTRY)	TOTAL GOODS HANDLED (TONNES)
Rotterdam (Netherlands)	350,000,000
Singapore (Singapore)	290,000,000
Chiba (Japan)	173,700,000
Kobe (Japan)	171,000,000
Hong Kong (China)	147,000,000
Houston (US)	142,000,000

SEA AND AIR FACTS

• The world's largest ship, the tanker *Jahre Viking*, is 458 m long.

• The Boeing 747-700, the largest airliner, has a wingspan of 64.4 m.

COUNTRIES WITH HIGHEST TONNAGE		
COUNTRY OF SHIPS	NUMBER	TOTAL GRT*
Panama	5,564	57,618,623
Liberia	1,611	53,918,534
Greece	1,929	29,134,435
Japan	9,950	24,247,525
Cyprus	1,591	22,842,009
Bahamas	1,121	21,224,164
Norway	785	19,383,417
Russia	5,335	16,813,761
China	2,501	14,944,999
Malta	1,037	14,163,357

* GRT or Gross Registered Tonnage is the cubic capacity of a ship (1 ton = 100 cubic ft)

COUNTRIES WITH THE LONGEST INLAND WATERWAY NETWORKS*		
COUNTRY	KM	MILES
China	138,600	86,122
Russia	100,000	62,137
Brazil	50,000	31,069
US**	41,009	25,482
Indonesia	21,579	13,409
Vietnam	17,702	11,000
India	16,180	10,054
Zaire	15,000	9,321
France	14,932	9,278
Colombia	14,300	8,886

* Canals and navigable rivers
** Excluding the Great Lakes

LONGEST SHIP CANALS					
CANAL	LOCATION	DATE BUILT	LENGTH KM	MILES	
Suez	Links the Red Sea with the Mediterranean Sea	1869	174	108	
Kiel	Links the North Sea with the Baltic Sea, Germany	1895	99	61	
Panama	Links the Atlantic Ocean and the Caribbean Sea with the Pacific Ocean	1914	81	50	
Manchester	Links inland UK canal systems	1894	57	35	

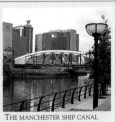

THE MANCHESTER SHIP CANAL

COMMUNICATIONS

COMMUNICATION IS a fundamental human concern. At present, the world is being transformed by a technological revolution that will communicate information across all linguistic and cultural barriers.

SAMUEL MORSE

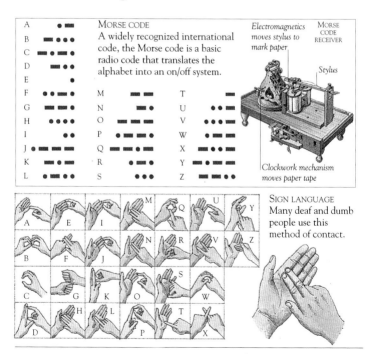

MORSE CODE

A widely recognized international code, the Morse code is a basic radio code that translates the alphabet into an on/off system.

Electromagnetics moves stylus to mark paper

MORSE CODE RECEIVER

Stylus

Clockwork mechanism moves paper tape

SIGN LANGUAGE

Many deaf and dumb people use this method of contact.

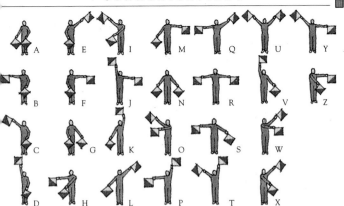

A E I M Q U Y

B F J N R V Z

C G K O S W

D H L P T X

SEMAPHORE
This system of signalling with hand-held flags is used as communication between ships at sea.

SATELLITES
Communications satellites that orbit the Earth make contact between countries quicker and easier. Radio waves from the caller are deflected via satellite to a receiver.

GLOBAL INTERNET
Information can now be sent instantly by computers on the growing global network known as the Internet.

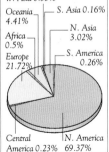

W. Asia 0.33%
S. Asia 0.16%
Oceania 4.41%
N. Asia 3.02%
Africa 0.5%
Europe 21.72%
S. America 0.26%
Central America 0.23%
N. America 69.37%

INTERNATIONAL IDENTIFICATION SYSTEM			
A	ALPHA	N	NOVEMBER
B	BRAVO	O	OSCAR
C	CHARLIE	P	PAPA
D	DELTA	Q	QUEBEC
E	ECHO	R	ROMEO
F	FOXTROT	S	SIERRA
G	GOLF	T	TANGO
H	HOTEL	U	UNIFORM
I	INDIA	V	VICTOR
J	JULIET	W	WHISKY
K	KILO	X	X-RAY
L	LIMA	Y	YANKEE
M	MIKE	Z	ZULU

ENGINEERING

HUMANKIND HAS USED construction to improve its habitat. Buildings are made for housing and to create working environments; roads, tunnels, and bridges allow easier movement across the surface of the land; dams harness nature's power to create electricity.

KEY MODERN ARCHITECTS			
NAME	DATES	NATIONALITY	BUILDING
Antonio Gaudi	1852–1926	Spanish	La Sagrada Familia, Barcelona, Spain
Frank Lloyd Wright	1867–1959	American	Guggenheim Museum, New York, US
Walter Gropius	1883–1969	German	Bauhaus, Dessau, Germany
Mies van der Rohe	1886–1969	German	Seagram Building, New York, US
Le Corbusier	1887–1965	Swiss	Nôtre Dame du Haut, Ronchamp, France
Richard Rogers	b.1933	British	Lloyds Building, London, UK

TALLEST BUILDINGS	
TOWERS	HEIGHT METRES (FEET)
KTHI-TV tower, North Dakota, US	629 (2,064)
KZFX-TV tower, Texas, US	615 (2,018)
TV tower, Devers, Texas, US	607 (1,991)

BUILDING AND LOCATION		
1	Petronas Twin Towers, KL, Malaysia	452 (1,483)
2	Sears Tower, Chicago, US	443 (1,453)
3	Jin Mao Building, Shanghai, China	420 (1,378)
4	World Trade Center, New York, US	417 (1,368)
5	Empire State Building, New York, US	381 (1,250)
6	Cental Plaza, Hong Kong, China	374 (1,227)
7	Bank of China, Hong Kong, China	368 (1,207)
8	T & C Tower, Kaoshiung, Taiwan	348 (1,142)
9	Amoco Building, Chicago, US	346 (1,135)
10	John Hancock Center, Chicago, US	344 (1,129)

PETRONAS TWIN TOWERS, KL, MALAYSIA

TALLEST DAMS

DAM	LOCATION	DATE BUILT	HEIGHT METRES	FEET
Rogun	Tajikistan	1989	325	1066
Nourek	Tajikistan	1979	317	1040
Grande Dixence	Switzerland	1962	285	935
Inguri	Georgia	1979	271	889
Vaiont	Italy	1961	265	869
Mica	British Columbia, Canada	1973	244	800

SUSPENSION BRIDGES WITH LONGEST MAIN SPAN

BRIDGE	COUNTRY	DATE BUILT	LENGTH METRES	FEET
Akashi Kaikyo, Huogo	Japan	1998	1,990	6,529
Great Belt East	Denmark	1997	1,624	5,328
Jiangyin	China	1998	1624	5,328
Humber	UK	1981	1,410	4,626
Tsing Ma	Hong Kong	1997	1,377	4,518
Verrazano Narrows	US	1964	1,298	4,258
Golden Gate	US	1937	1,280	4,199
Höga Kusten	Sweden	1997	1,210	3,970

CIVIL ENGINEERING RECORDS

TITLE	STRUCTURE	SIZE
Longest road	Pan American Highway	24,140 km
Longest tunnel	New York City / W. Delaware, water supply tunnel, US	169 km
Longest walled structure	The Great Wall of China	2,350 km
Largest dome	Louisiana Superdrome, US	207 m
Deepest mine shaft	Western Deep Levels Gold Mine, South Africa	3,777 m
Deepest bore hole	Kola Peninsula, Russia	12,400 m+
Longest oil pipeline	Alberta, Canada/ New York	2,856 km
Communications cable	ANZCAN telecom. cable	15,151 km

GOLDEN GATE BRIDGE

FACT BOX

• Over 2,500,000 m³ of stone was used to construct Egypt's Great Pyramid of Khufu.

• The US Pentagon has more than 27 km (17 miles) of corridors.

• The largest shopping centre in the world, West Edmonton Mall, Alberta, Canada, is as big as 90 football fields.

THE ELECTRONIC BRAIN

COMPUTERS SIMPLIFY COMPLEX TASKS into calculations that can be performed quickly. Capable of storing large amounts of information for easy access, they have revolutionized the world of work. Computer performance has so increased, that we are in an age where the electronic brain will soon rival our own.

Monitor

THE BASIC COMPUTER
Computers are made up of simple, interactive components that allow programs to be run.

Microprocessor: carries out a program's instructions

Card systems for extra input

ROM (Read-Only Memory): permanently stored program to make computer ready for use

RAM (Random-Access Memory): stores programs being run

Hard disk

Mouse

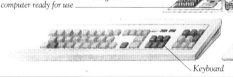

Keyboard

TIMELINE
1945 ENIAC (Electronic Numerical Integrator and Calculator) first built in the US.

ENIAC

1948 Manchester Mark I, the first stored-program (RAM) computer is built in the UK. Filling a room the size of a small office, it performs about 500 operations per second.

1958 US engineer Jack Kilby uses semiconductor material to make the first microchip (integrated circuit), using a semiconductor.

MICROCHIP

ARTIFICIAL INTELLIGENCE (AI) Scientists are developing AI to produce thinking computers. The difficulty lies in translating knowledge based on experience and intuition into a mathematical computer logic.

FACT BOX

• The CM-5, the fastest computer, can perfom 131 billion operations per second.

• Computer viruses are programs designed to destroy information in a computer's memory.

• Computers store data in binary: the electrical pulse is either on or off.

COMPUTER LANGUAGES

YEAR	LANGUAGE	MAIN USE	ORIGIN OF NAME
1954	Fortran	Scientific	**Formula translator**
1956	Lisp	Artificial intelligence	**List** processor
1959	Cobol	Business	**Common business oriented language**
1960	Algol	Scientific	**Algorithimic language**
1962	APL	Scientific modelling	**A programming language**
1964	PL/1	Business	**Programming language 1**
1965	Basic	Education	**Beginner's all-purpose symbolic instruction code**
1971	Pascal	Education	**Blaise Pascal**
1980	Ada	Military, all purpose	Ada Augusta, Lady Lovelace
1995	Visual objects	Database Access	**Visual Object** orientated program

BINARY CODE

ROMAN	DECIMAL	BINARY	HEX.
I	1	1	1
II	2	10	2
III	3	11	3
IV	4	100	4
V	5	101	5
VI	6	110	6
VII	7	111	7
VIII	8	1000	8
IX	9	1001	9
X	10	1010	A

1964 BASIC (Beginners All-Purpose Symbolic Instruction Code), the popular programming language, is created by professors at Dartmouth College, US.

1971 Intel 4004, the first microprocessor chip, is produced in the US. It performs 60,000 operations per second. 1977 Mass-produced computers appear.

1990 IBM Pentium PC produced. It can perform 112 million instructions per second.

PERSONAL COMPUTER

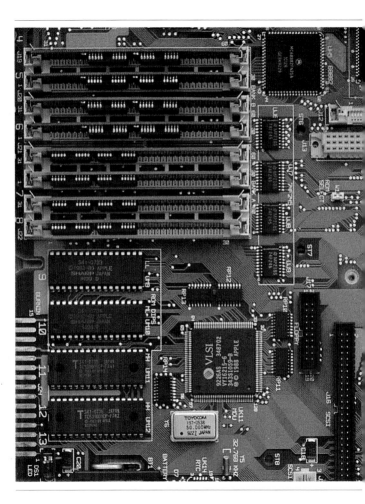

SCIENCE

SCIENTIFIC MILESTONES 76
THE PERIODIC TABLE 78
SCIENTIFIC UNITS 80
LIGHT AND SOUND 82
FOOD AND NUTRITION 84

SCIENTIFIC MILESTONES

FOR CENTURIES, SCIENTISTS have tested their ideas about the physical universe. The discoveries they have made have evolved into a body of knowledge that has revolutionized life on Earth, and led to inventions that have shaped modern civilization.

1620 – 1665	1776 – 1800	1803 – 1833

• 1620s English philosopher Francis Bacon proposes modern scientific method.

•1638 Italian scientist Galileo Galilei, the first person to use a telescope, founds mechanics (the study of force and motion).

1638
GALILEO'S
TELESCOPE

•1661 Irish scientist Robert Boyle realizes nature of chemical elements and compounds.

• 1665 English mathematician Isaac Newton formulates the laws of motion and of gravitation.

• c.1665 English physicist Robert Hooke develops the microscope.

• 1776 English chemist Henry Cavendish discovers hydrogen.

• 1770s French physicist Charles Coulomb studies electrostatic forces.

• 1779 French chemist Antoine Lavoisier names oxygen and shows its role in burning.

• 1799 Italian chemist Alessandro Volta invents his "voltaic pile" – the world's first battery.

• 1800 French physicist André Marie Ampère explores link between electric current and voltage.

1799
VOLTAIC PILE
BATTERY

• 1803 Englishman John Dalton proposes modern atomic theory.

• 1807–8 British chemist Humphrey Davy discovers potassium, sodium, magnesium, barium, and strontium.

• 1811 Italian Amedeo Avogadro formulates law stating that equal volumes of different gases contain the same number of particles.

• 1831 English scientist Michael Faraday and American scientist Joseph Henry discover how to use magnetism to create electricity.

• 1833 English physicist Michael Faraday discovers the laws of electrolysis.

1833
FARADAY'S RING

1843 – 1896	1897 – 1932	1938 – 1999
• 1843 English scientist James Joule describes relationship between heat, power, and work. • 1859 Belgian engineer Étienne Lenoir invents the internal combustion engine.	• 1897 British physicist Joseph John Thompson discovers the electron. • 1898 Polish-French chemists Marie Curie and Pierre Curie isolate radium and polonium. • 1900 German physicist Max Planck proposes quantum theory. • 1905 German-born physicist Albert Einstein publishes his *Special Theory of Relativity*.	• 1938 German scientist Otto Hahn and Austrian physicist Lise Meitner discover nuclear fission. • 1946 American scientist Willard Frank Libby invents the carbon-dating process. • 1960 American physicist Theodore Maiman makes first laser. • 1964 American physicist Murray Gell-Mann proposes existence of quarks, the smallest particles of matter. • 1986 Superconductors – substances with very low electrical resistance – are proposed. • 1990 Satellite discovery of ripples in background radiation supports Big Bang theory of origin of the Universe. • 1997 Scientists in Scotland produce the first clone of an adult animal – Dolly the Sheep.

1859 INTERNAL COMBUSTION ENGINE

• 1869 Russian schoolteacher Dmitri Mendeleyev classifies elements into groups by atomic weight, devising the periodic table.
• 1888 German physicist Heinrich Hertz establishes the existence of radio waves.
• 1894 Italian inventor Guglielmo Marconi makes the first radio communication.
• 1895 German physicist Wilhelm Roentgen discovers X-rays.
• 1896 French physicist Antoine-Henri Becquerel discovers the effects of radioactivity.

1905 ALBERT EINSTEIN

• 1909 American chemist Leo Henrick Baekeland invents "Bakelite" plastic.
• 1911 New Zealand-born physicist Ernest Rutherford discovers the atomic nucleus.
• 1931 German physicist Ernst Ruska invents the electron microscope.
• 1932 British physicist James Chadwick discovers the neutron.

1990 THE EXPANDING UNIVERSE

THE PERIODIC TABLE

CERTAIN ELEMENTS SHARE similar chemical properties and atomic structures. These similarities become clear when all the known elements are set out in a chart called the periodic table. This chart arranges elements into "groups"(columns) and "periods"(rows) and atomic structures. As the atomic number increases along each period, the chemical properties of the element gradually change.

GROUP 1	GROUP II	3	4	5	6	7	8	9
1 **H** Hydrogen								
3 **Li** Lithium	4 **Be** Beryllium							
11 **Na** Sodium	12 **Mg** Magnesium							
19 **K** Potassium	20 **Ca** Calcium	21 **Sc** Scandium	22 **Ti** Titanium	23 **V** Vanadium	24 **Cr** Chromium	25 **Mn** Manganese	26 **Fe** Iron	27 **Co** Cobalt
37 **Rb** Rubidium	38 **Sr** Strontium	39 **Y** Yttrium	40 **Zr** Zirconium	41 **Nb** Niobium	42 **Mo** Molybdenum	43 **Tc** Technetium	44 **Ru** Ruthenium	45 **Rh** Rhodium
55 **Cs** Caesium	56 **Ba** Barium	57–71	72 **Hf** Hafnium	73 **Ta** Tantalum	74 **W** Tungsten	75 **Re** Rhenium	76 **Os** Osmium	77 **Ir** Iridium
87 **Fr** Francium	88 **Ra** Radium	89–103	104 **Unq** Unnil-quadium	105 **Unp** Unnil-pentium	106 **Unh** Unnil-hexium	107 **Uns** Unnil-septium	108 **Uno** Unnil-octium	109 **Une** Unnil-ennium

Atomic number

Chemical symbol

15
P
Phosphorus

Name of element

Lanthanides and Actinides are separated to give the table a better shape

57 **La** Lanthanum	58 **Ce** Cerium	59 **Pr** Praseo-dymium	60 **Nd** Neodymium	61 **Pm** Promethium	62 **Sm** Samarium
89 **Ac** Actinium	90 **Th** Thorium	91 **Pa** Protact-inium	92 **U** Uranium	93 **Np** Neptunium	94 **Pu** Plutonium

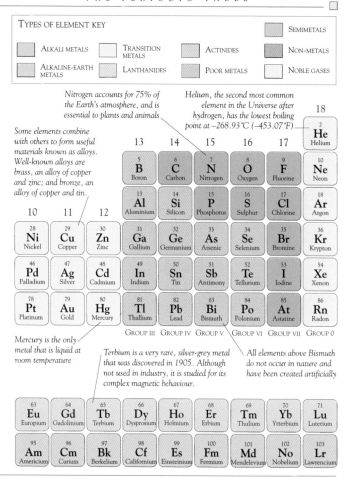

TYPES OF ELEMENT KEY

ALKALI METALS

ALKALINE-EARTH METALS

TRANSITION METALS

LANTHANIDES

ACTINIDES

POOR METALS

SEMIMETALS

NON-METALS

NOBLE GASES

Nitrogen accounts for 75% of the Earth's atmosphere, and is essential to plants and animals

Helium, the second most common element in the Universe after hydrogen, has the lowest boiling point at –268.93°C (–453.07°F)

Some elements combine with others to form useful materials known as alloys. Well-known alloys are brass, an alloy of copper and zinc; and bronze, an alloy of copper and tin.

Mercury is the only metal that is liquid at room temperature

Terbium is a very rare, silver-grey metal that was discovered in 1905. Although not used in industry, it is studied for its complex magnetic behaviour.

All elements above Bismuth do not occur in nature and have been created artificially

GROUP III GROUP IV GROUP V GROUP VI GROUP VII GROUP 0

SCIENTIFIC UNITS

IN AN ATTEMPT TO UNDERSTAND, describe, and quantify the processes of life, scientists have created diverse measurements. Units are standardized to avoid confusion. Concepts such as energy are measured using various units because energy is found in many different forms.

DISTILLATION USING A CONICAL FLASK

THE PH SCALE
The pH scale measures acidity or alkalinity with values of 0–14. Acidic substances dissolve in water to form sharp-tasting solutions that measure from 0–6. Alkalis dissolve to give soapy solutions with a scale of 8–14.

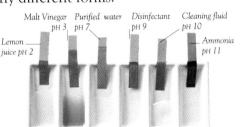

Malt Vinegar pH 3 Purified water pH 7 Disinfectant pH 9 Cleaning fluid pH 10

Lemon juice pH 2

Ammonia pH 11

ELECTRICITY AND MAGNETISM				
QUANTITY	SYMBOL	UNIT	ABBREVIATION	EXPLANATION
Voltage	V	volt	V	A battery/ generator produces a voltage that makes current flow in a circuit.
Current	I	ampere	A	A current is a flow of charged particles, usually electrons.
Resistance	R	ohm	Ω	Resistance is the degree to which a conductor opposes the flow of current.
Energy	E	joule	J	One joule is used every second when 1 amp flows through a resistance of 1 ohm.
Power	P	watt	W	Power is a rate of work done/electricity used. 1 watt is equal to a rate of 1 joule per second.
Charge	Q	coulomb	C	A coulomb is the charge moved in 1 second by a current of 1 amp.

MINERAL HARDNESS
Moh's scale is a
measurement of
hardness that uses a
scale of 1 to 10 to
grade minerals.

*1 Talc: can
be crushed by
a fingernail*

*2 Gypsum:
scratched by
a fingernail*

*3 Calcite:
scratched by
a bronze coin*

*4 Fluorite:
scratched
by glass*

*5 Apatite:
scratched by
penknife*

*6 Feldspar:
scratched
by quartz*

*7 Quartz:
scratched by
hard steel file*

*8 Topaz:
scratched by
corundum*

*9 Corundum:
scratched
by diamond*

*10 Diamond:
scratched
only by diamond*

ENERGY UNITS

Unit	Joule equivalent
Joule (J)	
Watts (W)	1 J per second
Horsepower (Hp)	2,600,000 J
Calories (Kcal)	4,184 J
Kilowatt hour (kWh)	3,600,000 J

British physicist James Joule (1818–89) gave his
name to this SI unit. He discovered the first law
of thermodynamics (the conservation of energy).

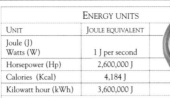

MAGNETIC FIELDS

Field	Tesla (unit of field measurement)
Weakest measured field	0.000000000008 T
Earth's field	0.00003 T
Powerful magnet	1 T
Highest field on record	30.1 T

KEY SCIENTISTS

BLAISE
PASCAL
Pascal gave
his name to
units of
pressure: one pascal (Pa)
is one newton per m².

HEINRICH HERTZ
The German physicist
demonstrated the
existence of radio waves
whose unit of frequency
(one cycle per second),
is named the hertz (Hz).

ANTOINE BECQUEREL
The French physicist is
known for his discovery
of radioactivity and the
units measuring
radiation activity, the
Becquerel (Bq).

ISAAC
NEWTON
The unit of
force (that
required to accelerate a
mass of 1 kg at 1 m /sec) is
expressed in newtons (N).

LIGHT AND SOUND

BOTH LIGHT AND SOUND travel as waves through the air. Light forms part of the electro-magnetic spectrum, and every different colour has a different wavelength. Sound is also identified by different wave frequencies.

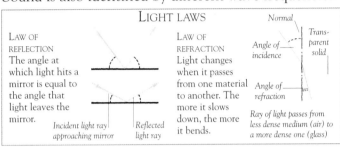

LIGHT LAWS

LAW OF REFLECTION
The angle at which light hits a mirror is equal to the angle that light leaves the mirror.

Incident light ray approaching mirror

Reflected light ray

LAW OF REFRACTION
Light changes when it passes from one material to another. The more it slows down, the more it bends.

Normal

Angle of incidence

Trans-parent solid

Angle of refraction

Ray of light passes from less dense medium (air) to a more dense one (glass)

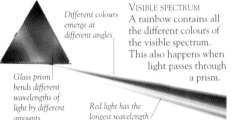

Different colours emerge at different angles

Glass prism bends different wavelengths of light by different amounts

Red light has the longest wavelength

VISIBLE SPECTRUM
A rainbow contains all the different colours of the visible spectrum. This also happens when light passes through a prism.

COLOUR WAVELENGTHS	
COLOUR	WAVELENGTH (NM)
Violet	370–440 nm
Blue	440–500 nm
Green	500–575 nm
Yellow	575–580 nm
Orange	580–610 nm
Red	610–720 nm

ELECTROMAGNETIC SPECTRUM
Different electro-magnetic waves have different ranges of wavelength.

Radio waves 100 km–1 mm

Television 0.5 m

Microwaves 0.3 m – 0.001 m

Decibel scale

Sound is created when objects vibrate. The vibrations cause the air to be compressed and contracted into sound waves. The loudness of a sound is measured in decibels.

SOUND FACTS

• Wavelengths can be as short as one nanometre (nm—one thousand millionth of a metre).

• Bats navigate in flight by emitting high-frequency squeaks.

• Sound travels at about 1,200 km/h (745 mph).

0 db: Sound you can only just hear

10 d: Someone whispering 5 m (16 ft) away

80 db: Pneumatic drill, 20 m (66 ft) away

100 db: Loud rock concert

120 db: Aircraft taking off 100 m (330 ft) away

130 db: Risk of hearing damage

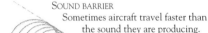

0 10 20 30 40 50 60 70 80 90 100 110 120 130 140 150

DECIBEL SCALE (db)

SOUND BARRIER

Sometimes aircraft travel faster than the sound they are producing. When this happens, a sonic boom occurs as compressed air at the front of the aircraft breaks to produce a shock wave.

Sonic boom released at speed of sound

SOUND SPEEDS		
Sound travels at different speeds through different materials.		
MATERIAL	SPEED	
	M/SEC	FT/SEC
Rubber	54	177
Air (0°C)	334	1,096
Air (100°C)	366	1,201
Water	1,284	4,213
Mercury	1,452	4,764
Wood	3,580	12,631
Iron/Glass	5,000	16,404

Infra-red 0.0005 m

Visible light 5 x 10⁻⁷m

Ultra-violet rays 1.0 x 10⁻⁸ m

X-rays 1.0 x 10⁻¹¹m

Gamma rays 1 x 1.0⁻¹³m

FOOD AND NUTRITION

WHAT WE EAT HAS a huge impact on our health. The study of diet is called nutrition, and it covers all aspects of the relationship of food to the maintenance of bodily functions and health.

VITAL FOOD COMPONENTS

MINERALS
These simple chemicals (e.g. calcium) are not made in the body but are required for its maintenance.

FIBRE
The indigestible part of fruit, vegetables, bread, and cereals, fibre aids normal bowel function.

CARBOHYDRATES
These are compounds of carbon, oxygen, and hydrogen, such as starch and sugar, that provide energy.

FATS
These supply concentrated energy. Also help form chemical "messengers", such as hormones.

PROTEIN
This is a substance the body needs for growth and repair. It is found in meat, fish, cheese, and beans.

MAIN VITAMIN SOURCES AND REQUIREMENTS		
TYPE OF VITAMIN	WHERE FOUND	REQUIRED FOR
Vitamin A	Liver, fish-liver oils, egg yolk, and yellow-orange coloured fruit and vegetables	Growth, healthy eyes and skin, fighting infection.
Vitamin B$_1$ (Thiamine)	Whole grains (wholemeal bread and pasta) brown rice, liver, beans, peas, and eggs	Healthy functioning of nervous and digestive systems.
Vitamin B$_2$ (Riboflavin)	Milk, liver, cheese, eggs, green vegetables, brewers yeast, whole grains, and wheatgerm	Metabolism of protein, fat, and carbohydrates. Keeps tissues healthy.
Vitamin B$_3$ (Niacin)	Liver, lean meats, poultry, fish, nuts, and dried beans	Plentiful energy and healthy, clear skin.
Vitamin B$_6$ (Pyridoxine)	Liver, poultry, pork, fish, bananas, potatoes, dried beans, and most fruit and vegetables	Metabolism of protein and production of red blood cells.
Vitamin C	Citrus fruit, strawberries, and potatoes	Healthy skin, teeth, bones, and tissues, and for fighting disease.
Vitamin D	Oily fish (e.g. salmon), liver, eggs, cod-liver oil, and some cereals	The absorption of calcium and phosphates.
Vitamin E	Margarine, whole grain cereals, and nuts	Formation of new red blood cells. Protection of cell linings in lungs.

FOOD SUPPLY

The "Dietary Energy Supply" (DES) is the amount of food available per person per day, and is measured in calories. This table compares the DES of some countries from around the world.

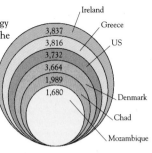

- Ireland 3,837
- Greece 3,816
- US 3,732
- Denmark 3,664
- Chad 1,989
- Mozambique 1,680

METRIC UNITS OF ENERGY							
JOULES TO CALORIES INTERNATIONAL		KILOCALORIES INTERNATIONAL TO KILOJOULES		CALORIES INTERNATIONAL TO JOULES		KILOJOULES TO KILOCALORIES INTERNATIONAL	
J	cal	kJ	kcal	cal	J	kcal	kJ
1	0.239	1	0.239	1	4.187	1	4.187
2	0.476	2	0.476	2	8.374	2	8.374
3	0.716	3	0.716	3	12.560	3	12.560
4	0.955	4	0.955	4	16.747	4	16.747
5	1.194	5	1.194	5	20.934	5	20.934
6	1.433	6	1.433	6	25.121	6	25.121
7	1.672	7	1.672	7	29.308	7	29.308
8	1.911	8	1.911	8	33.494	8	33.494
9	2.150	9	2.150	9	37.681	9	37.681
10	2.388	10	2.388	10	41.868	10	41.868
20	4.777	20	4.777	20	83.736	20	83.736
30	7.165	30	7.165	30	125.604	30	125.604
40	9.554	40	9.554	40	167.472	40	167.472
50	11.942	50	11.942	50	209.340	50	209.340
60	14.330	60	14.330	60	251.208	60	251.208
70	16.719	70	16.719	70	293.076	70	293.076
80	19.108	80	19.108	80	334.944	80	334.944
90	21.496	90	21.496	90	367.812	90	367.812
100	23.885	100	23.885	100	418.680	100	418.680

ENERGY CONVERSION

- To convert calories (cal) into joules (J), use the following formula:
  − x 4.187

- To convert joules (J) into calories (cal), use the following formula:
  − x 0.239

- To convert kilocalories (kcal) into kilojoules (kJ), use the following formula:
  − x 4.187

- To convert kilojoules (kJ) into kilocalories (kcal), use the following formula:
  − x 0.239

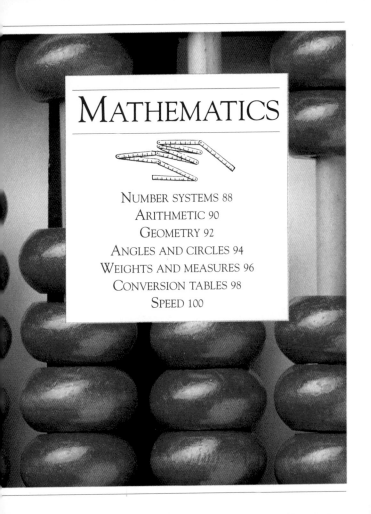

MATHEMATICS

NUMBER SYSTEMS 88
ARITHMETIC 90
GEOMETRY 92
ANGLES AND CIRCLES 94
WEIGHTS AND MEASURES 96
CONVERSION TABLES 98
SPEED 100

NUMBER SYSTEMS

HUMANKIND'S NEED TO COUNT led to the invention of numbers. Systems of counting and their component numbers are the language of mathematics, which has helped to quantify, describe, and explore many aspects of life.

BINARY SYSTEM

Our number system is based on the number 10, but number systems can be based on any number. The binary system is based on the number 2, and only uses the numbers 0 and 1.

BASE 10 NUMBER	BINARY NUMBER
1	1
2	10
3	11
4	100
5	101
6	110
7	111
8	1000

NUMBER SYSTEMS
Early civilizations organized counting systems once trade had advanced beyond barter. Each used different number symbols as dictated by the needs of their society. The Asian Indians and Mayan culture both invented the zero symbol independently.

SYMBOL SYSTEMS

NUMBER	ROMAN	ARABIC	CHINESE	BABYLONIAN	HINDU
0					
1	I	١	一	Y	٢
2	II	٢	二	YY	٩
3	III	٣	三	YYY	٣
4	IV	٤	四	YYYY	৪
5	V	٥	五	YYYY	५
6	VI	٦	六	YYYY	६
7	VII	V	七	YYYY	৩
8	VIII	٨	八	YYYY	८
9	IX	٩	九	YYYY	९
10	X	١٠	十	⟨	٩٠
50	L	٥٠	五十	⟨⟨⟨⟨	५٠
100	C	١٠٠	百	Y⟨⟨⟨⟨	٢٠٠
500	D	٥٠٠	五百	YYY Y⟩	५٠٠
1000	M	١٠٠٠	千	Y Y⟩	٢٠٠٠

MATHEMATICAL SYMBOLS			
SYMBOL	MEANING	SYMBOL	MEANING
+	Add (plus)	>	Greater than
−	Subtract (minus)	<	Less than
×	Multiply (times)	≤	Less than or equal to
÷	Divided by	≥	Greater than or equal to
=	Equal to	∞	Infinity
≠	Not equal to	%	Percent

$$3^2 \qquad 4^3 \qquad \sqrt{} \qquad \sqrt[3]{}$$

A number n squared is equal to n x n

This is shorthand for 4 x 4 x 4

The square root is often written without the 2

The cubed root is the opposite to the cube

NUMBER FACTS

• Negative numbers were first conceived in China in AD 200.

• The Greeks invented the "Golden ratio", an aesthetic number (1.618), and used it for building proportions in the Parthenon.

• The largest known prime number is 2^{756839} −1, which consists of 227,832 digits.

INDICES, SQUARES, AND ROOTS
The index (plural: indices) of a number n is the amount of times the number n is multiplied by itself. A number n squared = n^2 = n x n; n cubed = n^3 = n x n x n; and so on. The opposite of this is the root, i.e., a resultant number which, when multiplied by the power of the index, gives the original number n. If $^3\sqrt{n}$ = m, then m^3 = n; if $^2\sqrt{n}$ = k, then k^2 = n.

PRIME NUMBERS
A prime number is only divisible by itself and one, such as 13. Nine is not a prime, since it is divisible by three, as well as by itself and one.

FRACTIONS	STYLE TABLE		
The number above the line in a fraction is called the numerator, and the lower number is the denominator.	FRACTION	DECIMAL	PERCENT
	1/2	0.5	50%
	1/4	0.25	25%
	1/10	0.1	10%
	1/100	0.01	1%

PERCENTAGE	DECIMALS
Percent means "for each hundred" and signifies any fraction with a denominator of 100. So 1/2 is 50/100, or 50%.	Decimals are numbers written in base 10. Numbers after the decimal point are the number of tenths, hundreths, thousandths, etc.

SLICE AFTER SLICE
A cake divided into 8 slices means each slice equals 1/8.

ARITHMETIC

ROMAN POCKET ABACUS

ARITHMETIC IS THE BASIS of mathematics and initially falls into four categories: addition, subtraction, multiplication, and division. These operations form the core counting systems.

AN ELECTRONIC CALCULATOR

ADDITION

$$4 + 2 = 6$$

addend *addend* *sum*

MULTIPLICATION

$$4 \times 3 = 12$$

multiplicand *multiplier* *product*

SUBTRACTION

$$24 - 13 = 11$$

minuend *subtrahend* *difference*

DIVISION

$$44 \div 13 = 3 \text{ r } 5$$

dividend *divisor* *quotient* *remainder*

CACULATORS
Calculators range from the abacus to modern electronic models that perform mathematical operations instantly.

HOW TO USE
MULTIPLICATION TABLES
Simply measure off the desired number in the row and match it with the column numbers to give multiplication answers.

MULTIPLICATION TABLE												
COLUMN												
ROW	1	2	3	4	5	6	7	8	9	10	11	12
1	1	2	3	4	5	6	7	8	9	10	11	12
2	2	4	6	8	10	12	14	16	18	20	22	24
3	3	6	9	12	15	18	21	24	27	30	33	36
4	4	8	12	16	20	24	28	32	36	40	44	48
5	5	10	15	20	25	30	35	40	45	50	55	60
6	6	12	18	24	30	36	42	48	54	60	66	72
7	7	14	21	28	35	42	49	56	63	70	77	84
8	8	16	24	32	40	48	56	64	72	80	88	96
9	9	18	27	36	45	54	63	72	81	90	99	108
10	10	20	30	40	50	60	70	80	90	100	110	120
11	11	22	33	44	55	66	77	88	99	110	121	132
12	12	24	36	48	60	72	84	96	108	120	132	144

Simple and compound interest

Interest refers to money accrued as a credit or debt from a basic amount of borrowed capital. It is calculated as a percentage rate of the original amount. If a person places money in a bank, then the bank pays the customer interest on the money; if a person borrows money from a bank, then the person pays the bank interest.

SIMPLE INTEREST

This type of interest is calculated in respect to the original amount of money borrowed, or invested, which is called the principal.

$$\text{Total sum} = P(1 + \frac{i \times n}{100})$$

P is the principal,
i is the percentage of interest,
n is number of time periods.

EXAMPLE

If £100 is borrowed or lent for 1 year at 7% per annum (year), the total sum would be calculated as follows:
P = 100, R = 7, T = 1.
Total Sum = $100 + \frac{100 \times 7 \times 1}{100}$

$= 100 + 7$
$= £107$

COMPOUND INTEREST

While simple interest is paid only on the principal, compound interest is paid on the principal and the interest as it is earned and added onto the principal.

$$S = P \times (1+i)^n$$

P is the principal,
i is the periodic interest rate,
and n is the number of time periods.

EXAMPLE

If £100 is borrowed or lent for 2 years at 7% per annum (year), the total sum would be calculated as follows:
$= 100 \times (1 + 0.07)^2$
$= 100 \times (1.07)^2$
$= 100 \times 1.1449$
$= £114.49$

GEOMETRY

THE MATHEMATICAL STUDY of figures and solid shapes uses lines, angles, and surfaces to examine properties.

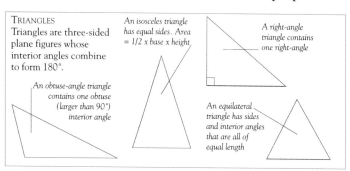

TRIANGLES
Triangles are three-sided plane figures whose interior angles combine to form 180°.

An isosceles triangle has equal sides. Area = 1/2 x base x height

A right-angle triangle contains one right-angle

An obtuse-angle triangle contains one obtuse (larger than 90°) interior angle

An equilateral triangle has sides and interior angles that are all of equal length

POLYGONS
These are shapes that have many (three or more) angles and sides.

Square: all sides and angles are the same length

Hexagon: polygon with six sides

Pentagon: polygon with five sides

Octagon: polygon with eight sides

Quadrilateral: four sided polygon

REGULAR POLYGONS		
NAME	NO OF SIDES	INTERNAL ANGLES
Triangle	3	60°
Quadrilateral	4	90°
Pentagon	5	108°
Hexagon	6	120°
Heptagon	7	128.6°
Octagon	8	135°
Nonagon	9	140°
Decagon	10	144°
Undecagon	11	147.3°
Dodecagon	12	150°

PLANE FIGURES

These are two-dimensional (flat) shapes, such as quadrilaterals or polygons, that are plane figures with three or more straight sides.

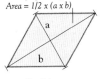

Rhombus: quadrilateral with sides of equal length
Area = 1/2 x (a x b)

Rectangle: quadrilateral with opposite sides of equal length that meet at right angles.
Area = base x height

Trapezium: quadrilateral with only two sides parallel. Area = 1/2 x sum of parallel sides x distance between them

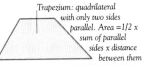

Parallelogram: quadrilateral with opposite sides of equal length. Area = a x b

SOLIDS

Solids are three-dimensional shapes. Polyhedrons are solids that have plane (flat) faces.

Cylinder: two circular faces, connected by a tube
Surface area = π x diameter x length. Volume π x radius² x length

Cone: Circular base, narrowing to a point, or apex. Volume = 1/3 x π x radius² x height
Apex

Rectangular block: volume = length x breadth x height

Tetrahedron: polyhedron with four triangles as faces

Sphere: globe-shaped figure with every point equidistant from the centre

Cubes: polyhedrons with 6 sides of equal length, shape, and area

Octohedron: tetrahedron with eight flat sides

Hemisphere: half of a sphere

Triangular prism: solid figure with two triangular ends. Volume = area of ends x distance between them

Square pyramid: tetrahedron with square base and four triangular sides

Spheroid: egg-shaped figure

ANGLES AND CIRCLES

AN ANGLE IS THE MEASURE of space between two lines
on a flat surface (or three planes in a solid) that join
at a common point. Angles are measured in degrees
(°), or radians. When one angle has passed through
360°, it has formed a complete circle.

ANATOMY OF A CIRCLE
A circle is a closed curve on which
all points are equidistant from the
centre. Its diameter passes from one
side to another through this centre
point. Its ratio to the circumference
is a expressed by Pi (π) or 3.141592.

*Chord: a straight
line joining any
two points on the
circumference*

*Segment: part of a
circle between a chord
and the circumference*

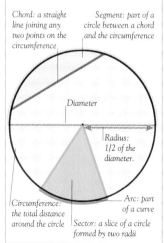

Diameter

*Radius:
1/2 of the
diameter.*

*Circumference:
the total distance
around the circle*

*Arc: part
of a curve*

*Sector: a slice of a circle
formed by two radii*

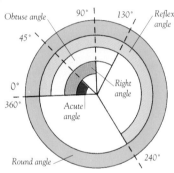

Obtuse angle 90° 130° *Reflex
angle*

45°

0°

360°

*Right
angle*

*Acute
angle*

Round angle 240°

DEGREES OF A CIRCLE
The hands of a clock form an angle
between each other. As they move
apart, that angle increases.

TYPES OF ANGLE	
TYPE	MEASUREMENT
Acute angle	angle between 0° – 90°
Right angle	angle measures exactly 90°
Obtuse angle	angle between 90° – 180°
Reflex angle	angle between 180° – 360°
Complementary angles	2 angles that add up to 90°
Supplementary angles	2 angles that add up to 180°
Conjugate angles	2 angles that add up to 360°

Trigonometry

Trigonometry is used to solve problems concerning right-angled triangles. Since there is a fixed angle, ratios exist that affect the relationships of the other angles and the lengths of their sides.

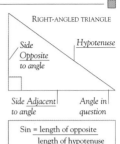

Hypotenuse

Side Opposite to angle

Side Adjacent to angle

Angle in question

$$Sin = \frac{\text{length of opposite}}{\text{length of hypotenuse}}$$

$$Cos = \frac{\text{length of adjacent}}{\text{length of hypotenuse}}$$

$$Tan = \frac{\text{length of opposite}}{\text{length of adjacent}}$$

TRIGONOMETRY CALCULATION
To find the height of the tower, multiply the tangent (tan) of the angle from the point of the observer to the top of the tower (40°) by the distance from the tower (659 m). This gives a height of 583 m.

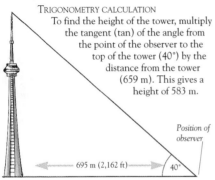

Position of observer

695 m (2,162 ft)

40°

TRIGONOMIC RATIOS
Since the hypotenuse always remains opposite the right angle, then this forms the basis for the ratios of angles and sides.

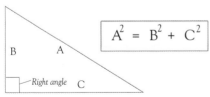

$$A^2 = B^2 + C^2$$

B   A

Right angle   C

PYTHAGORAS' THEOREM
This states that for any right-angled triangle, the squares of the two sides adjacent to the right angle (B and C) are equal to the square of the hypoteneuse (A, the longest side of the triangle).

MATHEMATICS FACTS
• The theorem that bears the name of the Greek mathematician Pythagoras was known by the Babylonians and Egyptians hundreds of years earlier.

• The terms *algorithm* and *algebra* come from al-Khwarizmi, the Arab mathematician.

WEIGHTS AND MEASURES

TWO MAJOR SYSTEMS OF MEASUREMENT exist: metric and imperial. Although some countries still use the older imperial system, scientists worldwide use metric.

THE SEVEN BASE SI UNITS

SI (Système Internationale d'Unités) is the standard system of units for scientists worldwide. There are seven base units, from which the other units are derived.

QUANTITY	SYMBOL	UNIT
Mass	kg	Kilogram
Length	m	Metre
Time	s	Second
Electric current	A	Ampere
Temperature	K	Kelvin
Luminous intensity	cd	Candela
Amount of substance	mol	Mole

IMPERIAL & USCS UNIT
Imperial units include the pound, mile, and gallon. With no scientific basis, it is a complex system. In the US, this system is called USCS (US Customary Systems).

STANDARD KILOGRAM

STANDARDS
Several units have precisely defined standards. This ensures that everyone means the same thing when stating measurements.

THE STANDARD SECOND
One second is defined as "the duration of 9,192,631,770 periods of the radiation corresponding to the transition between the hyperfine levels of the ground state of the cesium-133 atom."

THE STANDARD KILOGRAM
A standard kilogram is kept in carefully controlled conditions at the Bureau of Weights and measures at Sèvres, France.

THE STANDARD METRE
One metre is defined as "the length equal to the 1,650,763.73 wavelengths, in a vacuum, of the radiation corresponding to the transition between the levels 2p10 and 5d5 of the krypton-86 atom."

NUMBER TERMS GREAT AND SMALL*

PREFIX	SYMBOL	MEANING	PREFIX	SYMBOL	MEANING
tera	T	One million million	deci	d	One-tenth
giga	G	One thousand million	denti	c	One-hundredth
mega	M	One million	milli	m	One- thousandth
kilo	k	One thousand	micro	μ	One-millionth
hecto	h	One hundred	nano	n	One-thousand millionth

*Prefixes inserted before a unit signify multiples or fractions of that unit.

Adjustable jaw

MEASURING
SOLIDS
Calipers are used
to find the width of
solid objects.

LENGTH

METRIC	
1 millimetre (mm)	
1 centimetre (cm)	10 mm
1 metre (m)	100 cm
1 kilometre (km)	1,000 m
IMPERIAL	
1 inch (in)	
1 foot (ft)	12 in
1 yard (yd)	3 ft
1 mile	1,760 yd

MASS AND WEIGHT

METRIC	
1 gram (g)	
1 kilogram (kg)	1,000 g
1 tonne (t)	1,000 kg
IMPERIAL	
1 ounce (oz)	
1 pound (lb)	16 oz
1 stone	14 lb
1 hundredweight (cwt)	8 stones
1 ton	20 cwt

LIQUID MEASURES
Measuring jugs are used to
find the volumes of liquids.

MEASUREMENT FACTS

• France was the first country to adopt the metric system. King Louis XVI approved it in 1791, the day before he tried to flee the Revolution.

• China was the first country to use a decimal system. Wooden rulers divided into units of ten have been found and dated to the 6th century BC.

• In England, the length of the human top-thumb joint was a widely used measure that became the precursor of the inch.

AREA

METRIC	
1 square millimetre (mm²)	
1 square centimetre (cm²)	100 mm²
1 square metre (m²)	10,000 cm²
1 hectare (ha)	10,000 m²
1 square kilometre (km²)	1,000,000 m²
IMPERIAL	
1 square inch (in²)	
1 square foot (ft²)	144 in²
1 square yard (yd²)	9 ft²
1 acre	4,840 yd²
1 square mile	640 acres

VOLUME

METRIC	
1 cubic millimetre (mm³)	
1 cubic centimetre (cm³)	1,000 mm³
1 cubic metre (m³)	1,000,000 cm³
1 litre	1,000 cm³
IMPERIAL	
1 cubic inch (in³)	
1 cubic foot (ft³)	1,728 in³
1 cubic yard (yd³)	27 ft³
1 fluid ounce (fl oz)	
1 pint (pt)	20 fl oz
1 gallon (gal)	8 pt

CONVERSION TABLES

LENGTH CONVERSION

TO CONVERT:	INTO:	MULTIPLY BY:
IMPERIAL	METRIC	
Inches	Centimetres	2.54
Feet	Metres	0.3048
Yards	Metres	0.9144
Miles	Kilometres	1.6093
METRIC	IMPERIAL	
Centimetres	Inches	0.3937
Metres	Feet	3.2808
Metres	Yards	1.0936
Kilometres	Miles	0.6214
Metres	Furlongs	0.005
Metres	Fathoms	0.547
Kilometres	Nautical miles	0.54
Metres	Chains	0.0497

VOLUME CONVERSION

TO CONVERT:	INTO:	MULTIPLY BY:
IMPERIAL	METRIC	
Cubic inches	Cubic cm (ml)	16.3871
Cubic feet	Litres	28.3169
Cubic yards	Cubic metres	0.7646
Fluid ounces	Cubic cm (ml)	28.413
Pints	Litres	0.5683
Gallons	Litres	4.5461
METRIC	IMPERIAL	
Cubic cm	Cubic inches	0.061
(millilitres)	Fluid ounces	0.0352
Litres	Cubic feet	0.0353
Cubic metres	Cubic yards	1.308
Litres	Pints	1.7598
	Gallons	0.22

AREA CONVERSION

TO CONVERT:	INTO:	MULTIPLY BY:
IMPERIAL	METRIC	
Sq inches	Sq centimetres	6.4516
Sq feet	Sq metres	0.0929
Sq yards	Sq metres	0.8361
Acres	Hectares	0.4047
Sq miles	Sq kilometres	2.59
METRIC	IMPERIAL	
Sq centimetres	Sq inches	0.155
Sq metres	Sq feet	10.7639
Sq metres	Sq yards	1.196
Hectares	Acres	2.4711
Sq kilometres	Sq miles	0.3861

MASS AND WEIGHT CONVERSIONS

TO CONVERT:	INTO:	MULTIPLY BY:
IMPERIAL	METRIC	
Ounces	Grams	28.3495
Pounds	Kilograms	0.4536
Stones	Kilograms	6.3503
Hundredweights	Kilograms	50.802
Tons	Tonnes	0.9072
METRIC	IMPERIAL	
Grams	Ounces	0.0352
Kilograms	Pounds	2.2046
	Stones	0.1575
	Hundredweights	0.0197
Tonnes	Tons	1.1023

COOKING MEASURES		
OBJECT	METRIC	IMPERIAL
1 thimble	2.5 ml	30 drops
60 drops	5 ml	1 teaspoon
1 teaspoon	5 ml	1 dram
1 desert spoon	10 ml	2 drams
1 tablespoon	20 ml	4 drams
2 tablespoons	40 ml	1 fl oz
1 wine glass	100 ml	2 fl oz
1 tea cup	200 ml	5 fl oz (1 gill)
1 mug	400 ml	10 fl oz (1/2 pint)

2.5 ML (1/2 TEASPOON)

OVEN TEMPERATURES			
GAS MARK	ELECTRICITY		RATING
	°C	°F	
1/2	120	250	Slow
1	140	275	-
2	150	300	-
3	170	325	-
4	180	350	Moderate
5	190	375	-
6	200	400	Hot
7	220	425	-
8	230	450	Very hot
9	260	500	-

FAHRENHEIT TO CELSIUS TO KELVIN								
°F	°C	K	°F	°C	K	°F	°C	K
-4.0	-20	253	32.0	0	273	68.0	20	293
-2.2	-19	254	33.8	1	274	69.8	21	294
-0.4	-18	255	35.6	2	275	71.6	22	295
1.4	-17	256	37.4	3	276	73.4	23	296
3.2	-16	257	39.2	4	277	75.2	24	297
5.0	-15	258	41.0	5	278	77.0	25	298
6.8	-14	259	42.8	6	279	78.8	26	299
8.6	-13	260	44.6	7	280	80.6	27	300
10.4	-12	261	46.4	8	281	82.4	28	301
12.2	-11	262	48.2	9	282	84.2	29	302
14.0	-10	263	50.0	10	283	86.0	30	303
15.8	-9	264	51.8	11	284	87.8	31	304
17.6	-8	265	53.6	12	285	89.6	32	305
19.4	-7	266	55.4	13	286	91.4	33	306
21.2	-6	267	57.2	14	287	93.2	34	307
23.0	-5	268	59.0	15	288	95.0	35	308
24.8	-4	269	60.8	16	289	96.8	36	309
26.6	-3	270	62.6	17	290	98.6	37	310
28.4	-2	271	64.4	18	291	100.4	38	311
30.2	-1	272	66.2	19	292	102.2	39	312

TEMPERATURES

• To convert Fahrenheit (°F) into Celsius (°C), use the following formula:
$°C = (°F - 32) ÷ 1.8$

• To convert Celsius (°C) into Fahrenheit (°F), use the following formula:
$°F = (°C × 1.8) + 32$

• To convert Celsius (°C) into Kelvin (K), use the following formula:
$K = °C + 273.16$

Thermometers measure temperature on Celsius and Fahrenheit scales

RACING YACHT

SPEED

AN INCREASE IN speed allows an object to travel faster and cover distances more quickly. For many animals, this may mean the difference between life and death. For humankind, being able to travel quickly is a luxury that allows us to make more of our lives.

KNOT CONVERSION		
To convert:	Into:	Multiply by:
Metric:		
Knots	km/h	1.852
Km/h	knots	0.540
Imperial:		
Knots	mph	1.151
Mph	knots	1.001
Knots	feet/sec	1.688

TABLE OF MECHANICAL SPEED RECORDS		
RECORD DESCRIPTION	VEHICLE NAME	SPEED KM/H
Land	*Thrust SSC*	1228
Water	*Spirit of Australia*	514
Air (by air launch)	X-15A	7,297
Land (unmanned)	US Air Force rocket sled	4,927
Air (by take off)	Lockheed SR17a Blackbird	3,530

X-15A

SPEED FACT BOX

• Peregrine falcons can reach 350 km/h (217 mph) in a dive.

• Airliner Concorde cruises at 2,179 km/h (1,354 mph).

SPEED CONVERSIONS		
To convert:	Into:	Multiply by:
Kilometres per hour	miles per hour	0.621
Miles per hour	Kilometres per hour	1.609
Metres per second		0.447
Metres per second	Miles per hour	2.237
Feet per second	Miles per hour	0.681

ANIMAL SPEEDS

Animals are capable of great speeds, which they use to chase prey or escape predators. By comparison, even the fastest human sprinters lag far behind.

FASTEST BIRD

Spine-tailed swift can reach a speed of 171 km/h (106 mph)

FASTEST ON LAND

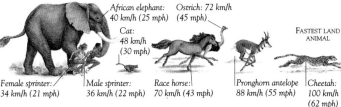

African elephant: 40 km/h (25 mph)

Ostrich: 72 km/h (45 mph)

Cat: 48 km/h (30 mph)

FASTEST LAND ANIMAL

Female sprinter: 34 km/h (21 mph)

Male sprinter: 36 km/h (22 mph)

Race horse: 70 km/h (43 mph)

Pronghorn antelope: 88 km/h (55 mph)

Cheetah: 100 km/h (62 mph)

FASTEST IN WATER

Male swimmer: 8 km/h (5 mph)

Dolphin: 48 km/h (30 mph)

Bluefin tuna: 74 km/h (46 mph)

Sailfish: 110 km/h (68 mph)

Gentoo penguin: 35 km/h (22 mph)

Tiger shark: 53 km/h (33 mph)

Marlin: 80 km/h (50 mph)

FASTEST FISH

WIND SPEED: THE BEAUFORT SCALE		
FORCE	SPEED	DAMAGE
Force 1	3 km/h (2 mph)	smoke drifts
Force 2	9 km/h (5 mph)	leaves rustle
Force 3	15 km/h (10 mph)	flags flutter
Force 4	25 km/h (15 mph)	small branches move
Force 5	35 km/h (21 mph)	small trees sway
Force 6	45 km/h (28 mph)	large branches move
Force 7	56 km/h (35 mph)	whole trees sway
Force 8	68 km/h (43 mph)	twigs break
Force 9	81 km/h (50 mph)	branches break
Force 10	94 km/h (59 mph)	trees blow down
Force 11	110 km/h (69 mph)	serious damage
Force 12	118 km/h (74 mph)	hurricane damage

WIND FACT BOX

• The world wind speed record of 371 km/h (231 mph) was recorded in 1934 on Mt Washington, US.

• Tornadoes are known to reach speeds of up to 450 km/h (280 mph).

• Over 1 month, Port Martin, Antarctica, had a mean wind speed of 105 km/h (65 mph).

PEOPLE

THE HUMAN BODY 104
THE SPOKEN WORD 106
THE WRITTEN WORD 108
FAITH SYSTEMS 110
SPORT 112
THE ARTS 114
CALENDARS 120

THE HUMAN BODY

EACH PERSON CONSISTS of a set of body systems. Each system uses organs that co-operate to make the body function. Cells, the basic units of life, divide and multiply to produce the different types of tissue used to make the body's organs. The body contains about 50 billion cells, which are continually being replaced.

The average human brain weighs 1.4 kg. and contains about 15 billion nerve cells. About 0.85 litres of blood pass through the brain every minute

Colour vision is so sensitive that some people can distinguish 300,000 different shades

The lungs contain over 300 million air sacs (alveoli) and have an average 5 litre air capacity

A person's heart beats about 37 million times a year, pumping the weight of 3000 tonnes of blood a day

The stomach contains hydrochloric acid to break down food and kill germs

The small intestine, used to absorb food, is around 2.8 m long

THE SKELETON
The skeleton consists of 206 bones (babies have over 300), which support the body and provide points of attachment for the muscles. They are lighter and five times stronger than a steel bar of the same weight. Bones also manufacture red blood cells and store calcium.

There are 27 bones in each hand

The femur (thigh bone) is the longest and strongest bone in the body. The smallest is the stirrup (stapes) bone in the ear

The total length of blood vessels in the average adult is 160,000 km

AVERAGE PEOPLE
The average vital statistics are as follows:
Height: man – 1.7 m
woman – 1.6 m
Weight: man – 73.5 kg
woman – 61.2 kg
Waist: man – 81 cm
woman – 73 cm
Hips: man – 96 cm
woman – 96 cm

THE MUSCULAR SYSTEM
Muscles carry out the body's movements. They work in opposing pairs and can contract to one-third their size. There are 639 muscles in the body, which account for 40% of its weight.

THE SKIN
Skin is the body's protective coating. It is waterproof, bacteria-proof and self-repairing. Nerve cells detect stimuli while over 3 million pores regulate body temperature. Skin also produces hair and nails from keratin, its protective protein.

THE CIRCULATORY SYSTEM
The circulation pumps blood around the body by means of the heart. A continuous circuit feeds oxygen to and from red blood cells via a network of arteries and veins. This network sends blood to the vital organs and carries chemical-rich plasma throughout the body.

THE NERVOUS SYSTEM
The nervous system is the communications network of the body. Stimuli send nerve impulses travelling at over 320 km/h across the body. Impulse messages are sent via the spinal cord to be translated and responded to by the brain.

THE SPOKEN WORD

PEOPLE USE LANGUAGES, organized systems of sound that express thought, to communicate with each other. It is believed that the many global dialects stem from a few root-languages: people in India and Iran share the same linguistic heritage as Europeans.

KEY

- Arabic
- Chinese
- English
- French
- Portuguese
- Russian
- Spanish
- Hindi
- Others

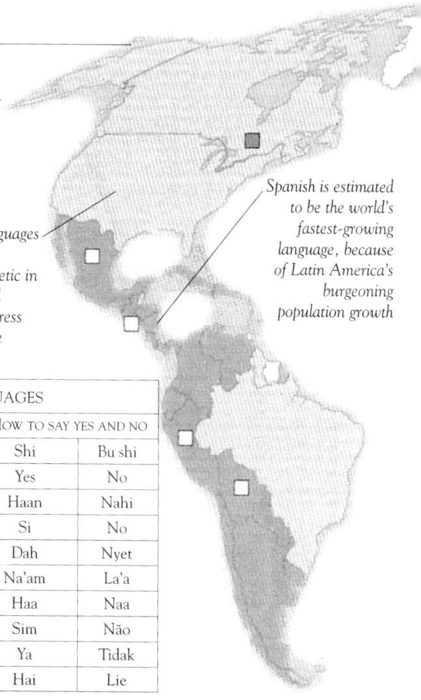

The Inuit of the Arctic circle speak "Inuktituit", a language belonging to the Eskimo-Aleut group that has around 60,000 speakers

Native American languages such as Chinook and Nookta are polysynthetic in that they use long and complex words to express the meanings of whole phrases

Spanish is estimated to be the world's fastest-growing language, because of Latin America's burgeoning population growth

MOST COMMON LANGUAGES		
LANGUAGE	NO. OF SPEAKERS	HOW TO SAY YES AND NO
Chinese (Mandarin)	1,093 million	Shi	Bu shi
English	450 million	Yes	No
Hindi	367 million	Haan	Nahi
Spanish	352 million	Si	No
Russian	204 million	Dah	Nyet
Arabic	202 million	Na'am	La'a
Bengali	187 million	Haa	Naa
Portuguese	175 million	Sim	Não
Malay-Indonesian	145 million	Ya	Tidak
Japanese	126 million	Hai	Lie

LANGUAGES OF THE WORLD
Between 5,000–10,000 languages and dialects exist in the world. This number is shrinking as indigenous dialects disappear in favour of unifying national languages. Some languages, like English, have become truly international.

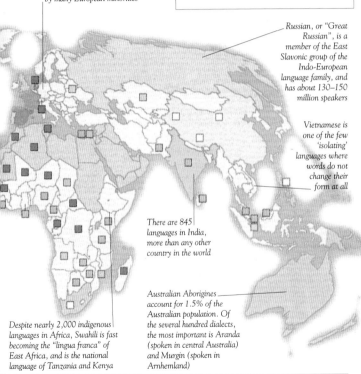

German has 75 million first-language speakers, the largest number in the European Union. It is spoken in Germany, Switzerland, and Austria, and by many European minorities

Russian, or "Great Russian", is a member of the East Slavonic group of the Indo-European language family, and has about 130–150 million speakers

Vietnamese is one of the few 'isolating' languages where words do not change their form at all

There are 845 languages in India, more than any other country in the world

Australian Aborigines account for 1.5% of the Australian population. Of the several hundred dialects, the most important is Aranda (spoken in central Australia) and Murgin (spoken in Arnhemland)

Despite nearly 2,000 indigenous languages in Africa, Swahili is fast becoming the "lingua franca" of East Africa, and is the national language of Tanzania and Kenya

THE WRITTEN WORD

WRITING BEGAN as pictures that related to objects or ideas. Later, writing systems arose that mirrored the spoken languages: logographic (signs for each word), syllabic (signs for syllables), and alphabetic (signs for each sound).

EAGLE   OWL

REED   SNAIL

ARM   SHUTTER

DOUBLE REED   WATER

CHICK   MOUTH

LEG   LION

HIEROGLYPHS
The ancient Egyptians used complex pictographic writing to adorn tombs and temples. The word 'hieroglyphics' means "sacred carvings".

CUNEIFORM
The Sumerians of Mesopotamia invented the oldest known script, cuneiform, around 3100 BC. The name refers to the wedge-shaped strokes used to form characters.

MEANING	3000 BC	2400 BC	650 BC
BIRD			
HAND			
HEAD			
REED			
WALK OR STAND			
WATER			

CHINESE
The Chinese language uses a logographic system that derived from unique pictograms. Concepts are conveyed using one or more pictographic symbols. For this, many characters are needed to express every word in the language. Chinese has 2–3,000 common characters, although the total number in use is about 50,000.

日 + 月 = 明
SUN MOON BRIGHT

一 上
ONE GO UP

小 天
LITTLE SKY

日 月
SUN MOON

心 去
HEART TO GO

汁 冰
JUICE ICE

魚 信
FISH LETTER

MAYAN

BURDEN VULTURE

WEST SOUTH

Of the 13 Mesoamerican writing systems identified, Mayan is the fullest. Symbols stood for objects or concepts, reflecting the Mayan preoccupation with time and the Universe.

FACT BOX

• "O", the oldest letter, has not changed its form since it was part of the early Phoenician alphabet in 1600 BC.

А Б В Г Д Е Ж З И Й К Л
М Н О П Р С Т У Ф Х Ц Ч
Ш Щ Ъ Ы Ь Є Э Ю Я О Ѵ

CYRILLIC

The Cyrillic alphabet is named after St Cyril who spread the Christian faith to the Slavonic peoples in AD 800.

HINDI

Of the 200 scripts derived from the Devanagari script, Hindi is used as the national written word.

अ आ इ ई उ ऊ
ऋ ए ऐ ओ औ क ख ग घ ङ च छ ज
झ ञ ट ठ ड ढ ण त थ द ध न प फ ब
भ म य र ल व श ष स ह

Individual alphabet letters translate every sound

PHOENICIAN	✕	⌐	⋀	⊿	⋺	Ⅰ	⊟	⊗	Ζ	✗	Ⅼ	Ϻ	Ч	‡	ⵔ	ᒋ	⌐	ⴷ	φ	ϙ	⟨	w	✝				
HEBREW	א	כ	ג	ד	ה	ו	ז	ח	ט	י	ר	ל	מ	נ	ס	ע	פ	צ	ק	ר	ש	ת					
EARLY GREEK	Λ	8	1	△	∃	Ⅰ	⊟	⊗	ⵔ	⅄	⅂	ᔕ	Ϻ	ᒍ	ⵔ	ⵔ	Ϻ	φ	ϙ	⟨	Χ						
CLASSICAL GREEK	Α	Β	Γ	Δ	Ε	Ζ	Η	Θ	Ι	Κ	Λ	Μ	Ν	Ξ	Ο	Π		Ρ	Σ	Τ	Υ	Φ	Χ	Ψ	Ω		
ETRUSCAN	Α	8	⅂	⌐	⋺	⅃	Ⅰ	⊟	⊗	Ι	⤙	⅃	Ϻ	Ϻ	⊞	Ο	⌐	Ϻ	φ	⟨	Τ						
ROMAN	A	B	C	D	E	F	G		H		I		K	L	M	N		O	P		Q	R	S	T	V	X	Y Z

DEVELOPMENT OF ALPHABETS

Basing their script on the Phoenician syllabary, the ancient Greeks invented the alphabet by introducing vowel signs that were separate from consonants. This became the source of modern alphabets.

FAITH SYSTEMS

RELIGIONS EVOLVED through people's desire to understand their place in the Universe and give meaning to their lives. Cultures express their beliefs in many different ways, reinforcing faith with the ritual of worship.

TOP SIX FAITHS	
FAITH	NUMBER OF FOLLOWERS
Christianity	1,833 million
Islam	971 million
Hinduism	733 million
Buddhism	315 million
Sikhism	13.5–16 million
Judaism	13–14.3 million

CHRISTIANITY

Christians believe in an historical figure called Jesus. They believe that, as the son of God, he brought teachings that were validated by his resurrection from the dead.

COMMUNION CUP

CHRISTIAN HOLY DAYS	
NAME	EVENT
Christmas	The birthday of Jesus Christ
Good Friday	Jesus is crucified on a cross
Easter	Jesus is resurrected from the dead
Pentecost	Descent of the Holy Spirit
Palm Sunday	Entry of Jesus into Jerusalem

ISLAM

Islam preaches that there is only one god, Allah. His followers, Muslims, study codes set out in the *Koran*, a divine text distilled by the prophet Muhammad.

BOOK OF ISLAM

ISLAMIC FESTIVALS	
NAME	EVENT
Mawlid al-Nabi	Birthday of Muhammad
Layl'at al-Quadr	Koran revealed to Muhammad
Id al-Fitr	Celebration of end of Ramadan
Id al-Adha	Celebration in memory of Abraham's sacrifice

HINDUISM

Hindus worship many gods, which reflects belief in life's diversity. Believers who live good lives are born again into a higher life.

BRAHMA

HINDU HOLY DAYS	
NAME	EVENT
Diwali	New Year Festival of Lights
Holi	Spring Festival
Jánmashtami	Birthday of Krishna
Shiva Ratri	Main festival of Shiva

BUDDHISM

 Siddhartha Gautama, the Buddha, was an historical figure who taught that desires are the cause of suffering. Many different forms of Buddhism exist in Asia.

THE BUDDHA

BUDDHIST HOLY DAYS	
NAME	EVENT
Wesak	Birthday of the Buddha
Dhammacakka	The Buddha's first sermon
Bodhi Day	Buddha's enlightenment
Parinirvana	The Buddha's liberation
Phagguna	Origin of life cycle

SIKHISM

 Sikhism originated in the Punjab area of the Indian subcontinent in 1500. It is based on a unity of god as taught by the ten Sikh gurus who established Sikhism.

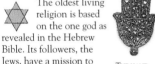
GOLDEN TEMPLE OF AMRITSAR

SIKH HOLY DAYS	
NAME	EVENT
Baisakhi	New year and formation of Khalsa
Diwali	Release from prison of Guru Hargobind, the sixth Guru
Guru Nanak	Birthday of the founder
Hola Mohalla	Three day festival held during Holi

JUDAISM

The oldest living religion is based on the one god as revealed in the Hebrew Bible. Its followers, the Jews, have a mission to transmit God's message.

THE HAND OF GOD

JEWISH HOLY DAYS	
NAME	EVENT
Hannukah	Festival of Lights
Pesach/Passover	Rescue from slavery in Egypt
Yom Kippur	Day of Atonement
Rosh Hashana	New Year

OTHER RELIGIONS		
NAME	FOUNDED	FAITH
Baha'i Faith	Persia, 19th c. BC	Worships one god who is at the root of all religions
Confucianism	China, 6th c. BC	Not based on worship of a god but on an approach to life that seeks to conform to the "Will of Heaven", life's ruling principle
Jainism	India, 6th c. BC	Established with the principle of "ahimsa", or non-violence, Jains believe in a soul but not in a god
Shintoism	Japan, 8th c. BC	Based on the worship of the gods and spirits of nature
Taoism	China, 4th c. BC	Balances life with the "Tao", the mystical power behind events
Zoroastrianism	Persia, 1000 BC	Based on a constant struggle between a good god (Ahura Mazda) and an evil god (Ahriman)

SPORT

ALTHOUGH THE ORIGINS of competitive sport are obscure, the ancient Greeks first held their Olympic Games in 776 BC. In 1896, the Olympics were revived, with most sporting development occurring since then. Today, organized sport takes place on both national and global levels.

OLYMPIC SYMBOL
The five interlocking rings symbolize Asia, Africa, Europe, America, and Australia.

SUMMER OLYMPIC GAMES venues					
YEAR	VENUE	YEAR	VENUE	YEAR	VENUE
1896	Athens, Greece	1932	Los Angeles, US	1972	Munich, Germany
1900	Paris, France	1936	Berlin, Germany	1976	Montreal, Canada
1904	St Louis, US	1948	London, UK	1980	Moscow, USSR
1908	London, UK	1952	Helsinki, Finland	1984	Los Angeles, US
1912	Stockholm, Sweden	1956	Melbourne, Australia	1988	Seoul, South Korea
1920	Antwerp, Belgium	1960	Rome, Italy	1992	Barcelona, Spain
1924	Paris, France	1964	Tokyo, Japan	1996	Atlanta, US
1928	Amsterdam, Holland	1968	Mexico City, Mexico	2000	Sydney, Australia

WINTER OLYMPIC GAMES venues					
YEAR	VENUE	YEAR	VENUE	YEAR	VENUE
1924	Chamonix, France	1960	Squaw Valley, US	1988	Calgary, Canada
1928	St Moritz, Switzerland	1964	Innsbruck, Austria	1992	Albertville, France
1932	Lake Placid, US	1968	Grenoble, France	1994	Lillehammer, Norway
1936	Garmisch, Germany	1972	Sapporo, Japan	1998	Nagano, Japan
1948	St Moritz, Switzerland	1976	Innsbruck, Austria	2002	Salt Lake City, US
1952	Oslo, Norway	1980	Lake Placid, US	During the two world wars, the
1956	Cortina, Italy	1984	Sarajevo, Yugoslavia	Olympics were not held.

CRICKET

Cricket originated in England and later spread to its colonies. The first test match was played in Melbourne in March 1877 between Australia and England. Today the sport is truly international, and the World Cup takes place every four years.

TEAM	TESTS	WINS
Australia	572	240
England	740	251
India	312	57
New Zealand	252	36
Pakistan	237	66
South Africa	209	53
Sri Lanka	76	9
West Indies	334	129
Zimbabwe	22	1

FOOTBALL WORLD CUP

YEAR	VENUE	WINNER
1930	Uruguay	Uruguay
1934	Italy	Italy
1938	France	Italy
1950	Brazil	Uruguay
1954	Switzerland	W Germany
1958	Sweden	Brazil
1962	Chile	Brazil
1966	England	England
1970	Mexico	Brazil
1974	W Germany	W Germany
1978	Argentina	Argentina
1982	Spain	Italy
1986	Mexico	Argentina
1990	Italy	W Germany
1994	US	Brazil

TENNIS TOURNAMENTS

TOURNAMENT	PLACE	SURFACE
Wimbledon	London, UK	Grass
United States Open	Flushing Meadow, New York, US	Artificial material
Australian Open	Nat. Tennis Centre, Melbourne, Australia	Synthetic
French Open	Roland Garros Stadium, Paris, France	Clay

To win the grand slam, is to hold all these titles simultaneously.

MAJOR GOLF TOURNAMENTS

TOURNAMENT	FIRST HELD	TOURNAMENT	FIRST HELD
British Open	1860	Ryder Cup	1927
US Open	1895	Curtis Cup	1932
US PGA	1916	US Masters	1934

Ryder and Curtis Cup are male and female team events.

SPORTING FACTS

• In 1954, Britain's Roger Bannister was the first man to run a sub 4-minute mile.

• The first man to run 100 m in under 10 seconds was Jim Hines of the US in 1968.

• In 1935, Jesse Owens of the US, set six Olympic records in only 45 minutes.

• The puck in ice hockey can reach speeds of up to 190 km/h (118 mph).

THE ARTS

PORTRAIT OF DR GACHET
This masterpiece was painted by Van Gogh in 1890 at the village of Auvers-sur-Oise, near Paris.

EVERY CULTURE EXPRESSES itself through art. From the earliest cave-paintings of prehistoric times to pop-art sculptures, humankind has invented many art forms. In western culture, art has moved beyond its expressive role in society to become a valued – and valuable – commodity. This has led to a cult of fine art, which is closely monitored by art historians.

POPULAR EUROPEAN GALLERIES	
ART GALLERY	VISITORS
Louvre, Paris	5,000,000
Prado, Madrid	1,828,058
Uffizi Gallery, Florence	1,020,972
Van Gogh Museum, Amsterdam	850,952
National Gallery, London	575,880
Alte Pinakothek, Munich	325,084

THE LOUVRE

MOST EXPENSIVE PAINTINGS SOLD AT AUCTION	
TITLE, ARTIST, DATE SOLD	PRICE IN US$
Portrait of Dr Gachet, Van Gogh, 1990	75,000,000
Au moulin de la galette, Renoir, 1990	71,000,000
Les noces de pierrette, Picasso, 1989	51,671,920
Irises, Van Gogh, 1987	49,000,000
La Reve, Picasso, 1997	44,000,000
Self portrait: Yo Picasso, Picasso, 1989	43,500,000
Au lapin agile, Picasso, 1989	37,000,000
Sunflowers, Van Gogh, 1987	36,225,000

KEY PAINTERS OF THE 20TH CENTURY

ARTIST	DATES	NATIONALITY	FAMOUS WORK	
Wassily Kandinsky	1866–1944	Russian	*Shrill-Peaceful Pink*	
Henri Matisse	1869–1954	French	*La danse*	
Pablo Picasso	1881–1973	Spanish	*Les demoiselles d'Avignon*	
Marc Chagall	1887–1985	Russian	*I and the Village*	
Salvador Dali	1904–1989	Spanish	*Premonition of a Civil War*	
Francis Bacon	1909–1992	English	*The Screaming Pope*	
Jackson Pollock	1912–1956	American	*Lavender Mist*	
Andy Warhol	1928–1987	American	*Marilyn*	SALVADOR DALI

KEY PHOTOGRAPHERS OF THE 20TH CENTURY

	ARTIST	DATES	NATIONALITY	FORM
	Man Ray	1870–1976	American	Experimental
	Edward Weston	1886–1958	American	Still-life
	Ansel Adams	1902–1984	American	Landscape
	Walker Evans	1903–1975	American	Documentary
	Bill Brandt	1904–1983	English	Documentary
	Henri Cartier-Bresson	1908–	French	Photojournalism
	Robert Capa	1913–1954	Hungarian	Photojournalism
ANSEL ADAMS	Richard Avedon	1923–	American	Portraiture

KEY SCULPTORS OF THE 20TH CENTURY

ARTIST	DATES	NATIONALITY	FAMOUS WORK	
Constantin Brancusi	1876–1957	Romanian	*Torso of a Young Man*	
Jacob Epstein	1880–1959	American	*Ecce Homo*	
Hans Jean Arp	1887–1966	French	*Eggboard*	
Henry Moore	1898–1986	English	*Mother and Child*	
Alberto Giacometti	1901–1966	Italian	*Suspended Square*	
Barbara Hepworth	1903–1975	English	*Figure of a Woman*	
Anthony Caro	1924–	English	*Verduggio Sound*	
Eduardo Paolozzi	1924–	Scottish	*Medea*	
Jean Tinguely	1925–	Swiss	*Homage to New York*	
Andy Goldsworthy	1956–	English	*Ice Sculptures*	HENRY MOORE'S *MOTHER AND CHILD*

Theatre, Film, and TV

The ancient Greeks are credited with inventing theatre. In the last hundred years, technology has transformed stage drama into cinema, a massive industry based on moving pictures. It has also found ways to beam pictures into people's homes, as television.

TECHNICOLOR CAMERA

WORLD TV VIEWING	
COUNTRY	HOURS PER WEEK
US	49.35
Italy	28.93
Hong Kong	28.70
Colombia	23.80
United Kingdom	23.80
Australia	21.98
Chile	17.50
China	10.59
Malaysia	10.50
World Average	19.67

FIRST COUNTRIES TO HAVE TELEVISION	
COUNTRY	YEAR
UK	1936
US	1939
USSR	1939
France	1948
Brazil	1950
Cuba	1950
Mexico	1950
Argentina	1951
Denmark	1951
Netherlands	1951

SHAKESPEARE FACTS

• William Shakespeare (1564–1616), the English dramatist, is the most influential writer to have lived.

• He wrote 36 plays, 154 sonnets, and 2 narrative poems.

• His *First Folio* was published in 1623.

MOST OSCARS® WON	
NAME OF FILM	AWARDS
Ben Hur (1959)	11
Titanic (1997)	11
West Side Story (1961)	10
Gigi (1958)	9
The Last Emperor (1987)	9
The English Patient (1996)	9
Gone With the Wind (1939)	8
From Here to Eternity (1953)	8
On the Waterfront (1954)	8
My Fair Lady (1964)	8

OSCAR®

KEY FILM DIRECTORS

NAME	DATE	NATIONALITY	KEY FILM
Fritz Lang	1890–1976	German	M (1931)
Jean Renoir	1894–1979	French	La règle du jeu (1939)
John Ford	1895–1973	American	Stagecoach (1939)
Sergei Eisenstein	1898–1948	Russian	Battleship Potemkin (1925)
Alfred Hitchcock	1899–1980	British	Psycho (1960)
Ingmar Bergman	1918–	Swedish	The Seventh Seal (1957)
Federico Fellini	1920–1993	Italian	La dolce vita (1959)
Satyajit Ray	1921–92	Indian	Pather Panchali (1955)
Stanley Kubrick	1928–	American	A Clockwork Orange (1971)
Steven Spielberg	1947–	American	E.T. (1982)

DIRECTOR'S CHAIR

HIGHEST GROSSING FILMS OF ALL TIME IN THE UK

FILM	YEAR	GROSS (£)
Titanic	1998	58,508,000
The Full Monty	1997	51,992,000
Jurassic Park	1993	47,140,000
Independence Day	1996	36,800,000
Men in Black	1997	35,400,000
Four Weddings and a Funeral	1994	27,800,000
The Lost World: Jurassic Park	1997	25,300,000
Ghost	1990	23,300,000

KEY 20TH-CENTURY PLAYWRIGHTS

NAME	DATE	NATIONALITY	PLAY
George Bernard Shaw	1856–1950	Irish	Pygmalion
Eugene O'Neill	1888–1953	American	Strange Interlude
Bertolt Brecht	1898–1956	German	Threepenny Opera
Samuel Beckett	1906–89	Irish	Waiting for Godot
Tennessee Williams	1911–83	American	The Glass Menagerie
Arthur Miller	1915–	American	Death of a Salesman
John Osborne	1929–1994	British	Look Back in Anger
Harold Pinter	1930–	British	The Caretaker

ORIENTAL THEATRE

• Japanese *kabuki* evolved in the late 17th century. It combines stylized acting with singing, dancing, and elaborate costumes and makeup.

• Indian *kathakali* trains its actors in the art of facial expression. This conveys all aspects of the story being told.

• Indonesian shadow theatre uses puppets, a narrator, and music to tell traditional folk tales.

JAVANESE SHADOW PUPPET

Music and dance

Both forms of expression have their origins in ancient religious ritual. In some parts of the world, people still dance themselves into trances to communicate with spirits; elsewhere, musical concerts and dance performances of many different kinds continue to keep audiences spellbound.

FAMOUS BALLETS

TITLE	CHOREOGRAPHER	FIRST DANCED
Les sylphides	Filippo Taglioni (1777–1871), Italian	1832
Nutcracker	Lev Ivanov (1834–1901), Russian	1892
Swan Lake	Lev Ivanov and Marius Petipa (1818–1910), French	1895
Manon	Kenneth MacMillan(1929–1993), British	1974

KEY DANCE STYLES

BALLET
Ballet uses formalized dancing, choreographed to music, to tell a story. Its main styles are modern, romantic, and classical.

TAP
Tap dance is characterized by tapping the heel and toe of the shoe on the floor to create rhythms.

CALYPSO
Caribbean carnivals were the birthplaces of calypso. This street dance is usually accompanied by steel-band percussion.

WALTZ
At first labelled immoral, the waltz changed dancing with its fast, turning movements and the close embrace of the dancers.

FLAMENCO
Derived from the old gypsy dances of southern Spain, flamenco is spontaneous and emotive.

WORLD DANCE STYLES

EUROPE
Many traditional European folk dances have their roots in religious ritual.

NATIVE AMERICAN
Dancing takes place at special ceremonies to win the goodwill of gods and ancestor spirits.

EAST ASIA
Dance is central to the main theatrical dramas. Japanese *gagaku* is one of the oldest traditional court dances.

SOUTHEAST ASIA
Highly trained artists perform slow, classical dances with complex hand movements.

AFRICA
Dance reflects the tribal roots of Sun and Moon worship, as well as hunt and fertility dances.

INDIA
Dancing re-enacts the ancient religious epics of gods and men.

INDIAN DANCER

KEY CLASSICAL COMPOSERS

NAME	NATIONALITY/ DATES	FAMOUS WORKS
Antonio Vivaldi	Italian, 1678–1741	*The Four Seasons*
Johann Sebastian Bach	German, 1685–1750	*Brandenburg Concertos, St Matthew Passion*
George Frederic Handel	German, 1685–1759	*The Messiah, Music for the Royal Fireworks*
Wolfgang Amadeus Mozart	Austrian, 1756–1791	*Piano Concerto in C major, Mass in C minor*
Ludwig van Beethoven	German, 1770–1827	*Symphonies No. 3, No. 5, and No. 9*
Franz Schubert	Austrian, 1797–1828	*Die Winterreise, Symphony No. 8 "Unfinished"*
Hector Berlioz	French, 1803–1869	*Symphonie fantastique, The Trojans*
Richard Wagner	German, 1813–1883	*The Flying Dutchman, The Ride of the Valkyries*
Peter Ilyich Tchaikovsky	Russian, 1840–1893	*Swan Lake, The Sleeping Beauty, The Nutcracker*
Claude Debussy	French, 1862–1918	*L'après-midi d'un faune, La mer, Images*
Arnold Schoenberg	Austrian, 1874–1951	*Transfigured Night, A Survivor from Warsaw*

KEY MUSICAL STYLES

FOLK MUSIC
This broad term applies to traditional, community-based music. Each society has its own form.

JAZZ
Born in the early 1900s, when musicians in the US began to improvise around popular music themes.

REGGAE
Beat music with a distinctive rhythm that originated in the West Indies in the early 1960s.

COUNTRY
The "white man's blues" of the US, country music now also embraces urban themes and styles.

BLUES
Basically simple, hugely influential, melancholic songs created by poor black minorities in the US.

POP
A 1950s term meaning any song or piece of music with mass appeal, usually with a danceable beat.

ROCK
A combination of various forms of black popular music with a heavy beat pioneered in the US and UK.

TECHNO
Based around a rapid 4/4 beat and electronic sounds, this style first became popular in the 1980s.

KEY OPERAS

TITLE	COMPOSER	FIRST PERFORMED
The Marriage of Figaro	Wolfgang Amadeus Mozart (1756–1791), Austrian	1786, Vienna, Austria
The Barber of Seville	Gioacchino Rossini (1792–1868), Italian	1816, Rome, Italy
The Ring of the Nibelung	Richard Wagner (1813–1883), German	1876, Bayreuth, Germany
La Bohème	Giacomo Puccini (1858–1924), Italian	1896, Turin, Italy

OPERA SINGER

CHINESE YEAR CYCLES

Each animal year repeats itself every twelve years.

RAT 1996	OX 1997

TIGER 1998	RABBIT 1999

DRAGON 2000	SNAKE 2001

HORSE 2002	GOAT 2003

MONKEY 2004	COCKEREL 2005

DOG 2006	PIG 2007

CALENDARS

THE PASSAGE OF TIME, beginning with the cycle of seasons, was civilization's first obsession. The ancient Maya devoted themselves to the "long count", using complex mathematics and astronomy. With these methods, other societies, too, have calculated their own calendar.

THE SEASONS		
NORTHERN HEMISPHERE	SOUTHERN HEMISPHERE	DURATION
Spring	Autumn	From vernal/ autumnal equinox (c. 21 Mar) to summer/ winter solstice (c. 21 Jun)
Summer	Winter	From summer/ winter solstice (c. 21 Jun) to autumnal/ spring equinox (c. 23 Sept)
Autumn	Spring	From autumnal/ spring equinox (c. 23 Sept) to winter/ summer solstice (c. 21 Dec)
Winter	Summer	From winter/ summer solstice (c. 21 Dec) to vernal/ autumnal equinox (c. 21 Mar)

NAMES OF THE DAYS	
DAY	NAME ORIGIN
Sunday	Sun day
Monday	Moon day
Tuesday	Tiw's day (god of battle)
Wednesday	Woden's or Odin's day
	(god of poetry and the dead)
Thursday	Thor's day (god of thunder)
Friday	Frigg's day (goddess of married love)
Saturday	Saturn's day (god of time)

SATURN

EXPLANATION OF CALENDARS

JULIAN/ GREGORIAN
The Julian calendar calculated the solar year at 365 days, divided into 12 months. In 1582, Pope Gregory XII adjusted a 10-day gap that had gathered between this calendar and the astronomical year.

ISLAMIC
The Islamic calendar is based on the lunar year and runs in cycles of 30 years. It begins with the year of Hijrah (AD 622), the flight of Muhammad to Medina.

CHINESE
The ancient Chinese calendar is based on the lunar year and has 12 months of alternatively 29 and 30 days. Each year is signified by an animal. A cycle passes through each one of the signs before returning to the start.

JEWISH
The Jewish calendar is based on the lunar year and consists of 12 months of 29 or 30 days. An extra month is added to 7 years of every 19-year cycle to bring the calendar back in time with the solar year.

JEWISH CANDLE HOLDER

MONTH OF THE YEAR

GREGORIAN	JEWISH	ISLAMIC	ZODIAC
(Basis : Sun)	(Basis: Moon)	(Basis: Moon)*	(Basis: Sun)
January	Shevat (Jan–Feb)	Jumada I	Capricorn (Dec 22–Jan 20)
February	Adar (Feb–Mar)	Jumada II	Aquarius (Jan 21–Feb 18)
March	Adar Sheni – leap years only	Rajab	Pisces (Feb 19–Mar 20)
April	Nisan (Mar–Apr)	Shaban	Aries (Mar 21–Apr 20)
May	Iyar (Apr–May)	Ramadan	Taurus (Apr 21–May 21)
June	Sivan (May–Jun)	Shawwal	Gemini (May 22–Jun 21)
July	Tammuz (Jun–Jul)	Dhu al-Qadah	Cancer (Jun 22–July 22)
August	Av (Jul–Aug)	Dhu al Hijja	Leo (July 23–Aug 23)
September	Elul (Aug–Sep)	Muharram	Virgo (Aug 24–Sep 22)
October	Tishri (Sep–Oct)	Safar	Libra (Sep 23–Oct 23)
November	Heshvan (Oct–Nov)	Rabi I	Scorpio (Oct 24–Nov 22)
December	Kislev (Nov–Dec)	Rabi II	Sagittarius (Nov 23–Dec 21)
	Tevet (Dec–Jan)	* No leap years – months change date each year.	

Index

A
acidity, 80
actinides, 79
addition, arithmetic, 90
Afghanistan, 42
Africa, 24, 44–7
agriculture, 51
air speed records, 100
air travel, 66
Alaska, 48
Albania, 41
Algeria, 44
alkali metals, 79
alkaline-earth metals, 79
alkalinity, 80
alphabets, 109
anatomy, human, 104–5
Andorra, 42
angles, 94-5
Angola, 45
animals, speeds, 101
Antarctica, 24
Antigua & Barbuda, 40
Arabic numbers, 88
architects, 70
area, 97, 98
Argentina, 38
arithmetic, 90–1
Armenia, 44
art galleries, 114
Artificial Intelligence (AI), 73
arts, 114–15
Asia, 24, 42–4
astronomy, 12–17

atmosphere, 21
atomic number, 78–9
Australasia, 47
Australia, 24, 47
Austria, 41
Azerbaijan, 43

B
Babylonian numbers, 88
Baha'i faith, 111
Bahamas, 39
Bahrain, 44
ballet, 118
Bangladesh, 43
Barbados, 40
battles, 59
Beaufort scale, 101
Becquerel, Antoine, 81
Belgium, 41
beliefs, 110–11
Belize, 39
Belorussia, 40
Benin, 46
Bhutan, 44
binary code, computers, 73
binary system, 88
birds, speeds, 101
blues, 119
body, 104–5
Bolivia, 39
bones, 104
Bosnia & Herzegovina, 41
Botswana, 45
brain, 104
Brazil, 38
bridges, 71
Britain, 40
  rulers, 54–5

Brunei, 44
Buddhism, 111
buildings, 70
Bulgaria, 41
Burkina, 46
Burma, 42
Burundi, 46

C
calculators, 90
calendars, 120–1
calories, 85
calypso, 118
Cambodia, 43
Cameroon, 45
Canada, 38
canals, 67
Cape Verde, 47
carbohydrates, 84
cars, 64
cells, 104
Celsius scale, 99
Central African Republic, 45
Central America, 38–40
cereals, 51
Chad, 44
Chile, 39
China, 42
  calendar, 121
  dynasties and republics, 57
  language, 108
  numbers, 88
  year cycles, 120
choreographers, 118
Christianity, 110
cinema, 116–17
circles, 94
circulatory system, 105

civil engineering, 71
climate zones, 30–1
coal, 50
Colombia, 38
colour wavelengths, 82
Commonwealth, 35
communications, 68–9
Communism, 53
Comoros, 47
composers, 119
compound interest, 91
computers, 72–3
Confucianism, 111
Congo, 45
constellations, 12–13
continents, 24
conversion tables, 98–9
cooking measures, 99
Costa Rica, 39
counting, 88–9
countries, 35, 38–47
country music, 119
cricket, 113
Croatia, 41
crude oil, 50
crust, Earth's, 28–9
Cuba, 39
cuneiform, 108
Cyprus, 44
Cyrillic alphabet, 109
Czech Republic, 41

D
dams, 71
dance, 118
days, 120
decibel scale, 83
decimal numbers, 89

degrees, circles, 94
Denmark, 41
deserts, 25, 31
diet, 84–5
Dietary Energy Supply
 (DES), 85
division, arithmetic, 90
Djibouti, 46
Dominica, 40
Dominican Republic, 39

E
Earth:
 climate zones, 30–1
 crust, 28–9
 land, 24–5
 as a planet, 16, 18–21
 time zones, 22–3
 water, 26–7
earthquakes, 28–9
eclipses, 14, 15
Ecuador, 39
Egypt, 45
 ancient, 56, 108
El Salvador, 39
electricity, 50, 80
electromagnetic
 spectrum, 82–3
electronics, 72–3
elements, 78–9
energy:
 calories, 85
 units, 81
 world resources, 50
engineering, 70–1
Equatorial Guinea, 46
Eritrea, 46
Estonia, 41

Ethiopia, 45
Europe, 24, 40–2
European Union, 35
Eurostar, 65

F
Fahrenheit scale, 99
faith systems, 110–11
fats, 84
festivals, 110–11
fibre, in diet, 84
Fiji, 47
film directors, 117
films, 116–17
Finland, 40
fish, 51, 101
flamenco, 118
folk music, 119
food, 51, 84–5
football, 113
fractions, 89
France, 40
fuels, 50

G
Gabon, 46
galaxies, 13
galleries, 114
Gambia, 47
gases, noble, 79
geological timescale, 20
geometry, 92–3
Georgia, 44
Germany, 40
Ghana, 46
global warming, 20
golf, 113
government, 34

Greece, 41
greenhouse effect, 20
Greenwich Mean Time (GMT), 22–3
Greenwich meridian, 22
Gregorian calendar, 121
Grenada, 40
Guatemala, 39
Guinea, 46
Guinea-Bissau, 46
Guyana, 39

H
Haiti, 39
Hawaii, 48
Heathrow Airport, 66
Hertz, Heinrich, 81
hieroglyphs, 108
Hindi script, 109
Hinduism, 110
holy days, 110–11
Honduras, 39
human body, 104–5
Hungary, 41

I
Iceland, 41
imperial measurements, 96–7
India, 42
indices, numbers, 89
Indonesia, 42
inland waterways, 67
interest, simple and compound, 91
International Date Line, 23
International Identification System, 69
Internet, 69

Iran, 42
Iraq, 43
Ireland, 41
Islam, 110
Islamic calendar, 121
islands, 25
Israel, 44
Italy, 40
Ivory Coast, 46

J
Jainism, 111
Jamaica, 39
Japan, 43, 57
jazz, 119
Jewish calendar, 121
Jews, 111
Jordan, 43
Judaism, 111
Julian calendar, 121
Jupiter, 16–17

K
Kazakhstan, 42
Kelvin scale, 99
Kenya, 45
kilograms, 96
Kiribati, 47
knots, speed, 100
Korea, 43
Kuwait, 44
Kyrgyzstan, 43

L
lakes, 27
land, 24–5
land speed records, 100
languages, 106–7

lanthanides, 79
Laos, 43
latitude, 19
Latvia, 41
Lebanon, 44
length, 97, 98
Lesotho, 46
Liberia, 46
Libya, 44
Liechtenstein, 42
light, 82
liquid measures, 97
Lithuania, 41
longitude, 19
lunar eclipse, 15
Luxembourg, 42

M
Macedonia, 42
Madagascar, 45
magnetic fields, 81
magnetic poles, 19
magnetism, 80
maize, 51
Malawi, 46
Malaysia, 43
Maldives, 44
Mali, 45
Malta, 42
Mars, 16
Marshall Islands, 47
mass, 97, 98
mathematics, 87–101
  angles and circles, 94–5
  arithmetic, 90–1
  conversion tables, 98–9
  geometry, 92–3

number systems, 88–9
speed, 100–1
weights and measures, 96–7
Mauritania, 45
Mauritius, 47
Mayan numbers, 88
Mayan writing, 109
measurements, 96-7
  conversion tables, 98–9
Mercalli scale, 29
Mercury, 16
metals, 79
metres, 96
metric system, 96–7
Mexico, 38
Micronesia, 47
Milky Way, 13
minerals:
  in diet, 84
  hardness, 81
  world resources, 50
Moh's scale, 81
Moldova, 41
Monaco, 42
monarchs, Britain, 54–5
money, interest, 91
Mongolia, 42
monsoon, 31
months, 121
Moon, 14, 15, 18
Morocco, 45
Morse code, 68
mountains, 25, 31
movies, 116–17
Mozambique, 45
multiplication, arithmetic, 90
muscles, 105
music, 118–19

Muslims, 110
Myanmar, 42

N
Namibia, 45
nations, 35, 38–47
NATO, 35
Nauru, 47
Nepal, 43
Neptune, 16–17
nervous system, 105
Netherlands, 41
New Zealand, 47
Newton, Isaac, 81
Nicaragua, 39
Niger, 45
Nigeria, 45
night sky, 12–13
noble gases, 79
non-metals, 79
North America, 24, 38
North Korea, 43
Norway, 40
number systems, 88–9
number terms, 96
nutrition, 84

O
oceans, 26, 27
oil, 50
Olympic Games, 112
Oman, 43
operas, 119
organizations, world, 35
Oriental theatre, 117
Oscars, 116
oven temperatures, 99

P
painting, 114–15
Pakistan, 42
Palau, 47
Panama, 39
Papua New Guinea, 47
Paraguay, 39
Pascal, Blaise, 81
people, 103–21
  arts, 114–15
  calendars, 120–1
  faith systems, 110–11
  human body, 104–5
  music and dance, 118–19
  spoken word, 106–7
  sport, 112–13
  theatre, film and TV, 116–17
  written word, 108–9
percentages, 89
periodic table, 78–9
Peru, 38
pH scale, 80
Philippines, 43
photographers, 115
pictograms, 108
plane figures, 93
planets, 16–17
playwrights, 117
Pluto, 16–17
Poland, 40
polar climate, 30
political world, 33–59
  American states, 48–9
  ancient rulers and
  dynasties, 56–7
  British rulers, 54–5
  nations, 38–47
  Russian rulers, 53

US presidents, 52
  wars, 58–9
  world resources, 50–1
polygons, 92
poor metals, 79
pop music, 119
Popes, 57
population, 34–5
ports, 67
Portugal, 41
presidents, US, 52
prime numbers, 89
protein, 84
Pythagoras' theorem, 95

Q
Qatar, 44

R
railways, 65
rainbow, 82
rainfall, 30–1
Red Crescent, 35
Red Cross, 35
reflection, law of, 82
refraction, law of, 82
reggae, 119
religions, 110–11
resources, world, 50–1
revolutions, 58–9
rice, 51
Richter scale, 29
rivers, 27, 67
road transport, 64
rock music, 119
Roman Empire, 57
Roman numbers, 88
Romania, 40

roots, numbers, 89
rulers:
  ancient history, 56–7
  Britain, 54–5
  Russia, 53
  US presidents, 52
Russia, rulers, 53
Russian Federation, 40
Rwanda, 46

S
St Christopher & Nevis, 40
St Lucia, 40
St Vincent &
  the Grenadines, 40
San Marino, 42
Sao Tome & Principe, 47
satellites, 69
Saturn, 16–17
Saudi Arabia, 42
science, 75–85
  food and nutrition, 84–5
  light and sound, 82–3
  milestones, 76–7
  periodic table, 78–9
  scientific units, 80–1
Scotland, monarchs, 54
sculptors, 115
sea transport, 66–7
seas, 26, 27
seasons, 18, 120
seconds, 96
seismometers, 29
semaphore, 69
semimetals, 79
Senegal, 46
Serbia, 41
Seychelles, 47

Shakespeare, William, 116
shapes, geometry, 92–3
Shintoism, 111
shipping, 66–7
SI units, 96
Sierra Leone, 46
sign language, 68
Sikhism, 111
simple interest, 91
Singapore, 44
skeleton, 104
skin, 105
skyscrapers, 70
Slovakia, 41
Slovenia, 42
solar eclipse, 14
solar system, 13
solids, geometry, 93
Solomon Islands, 47
Somalia, 45
sonic boom, 83
sound, 82–3
sound barrier, 83
sound speeds, 83
South Africa, 45
South America, 24, 38–9
South Korea, 43
Spain, 40
spectrum, 82
speed, 100–1
  sound, 83
spoken word, 106–7
sport, 112–13
square numbers, 89
Sri Lanka, 44
standards, measurements, 96
stars, 12–13
subtraction, arithmetic, 90

Sudan, 44
Sun, 13, 14, 18
Surinam, 39
suspension bridges, 71
Swaziland, 46
Sweden, 40
Switzerland, 41
symbols:
  mathematical, 89
  written word, 108–9
Syria, 43

T
Taiwan, 44
Tajikistan, 43
Tanzania, 45
Taoism, 111
tap dance, 118
techno music, 119
technology, 61–73
  communications, 68–9
  computers, 72–3
  engineering, 70–1
  transport, 62–7
tectonic plates, 28
television, 116
temperate climate, 30
temperatures:
  climate, 30–1
  conversion tables, 99
tennis, 113
Thailand, 43
theatre, 117
thermometers, 99
tides, 18
time:
  calendars, 120–1
  time zones, 22–3

Togo, 46
Tonga, 47
transition metals, 79
transport, 62–7
triangles, 92, 95
trigonometry, 95
Trinidad & Tobago, 39
tropical climate, 31
Tunisia, 46
tunnels, railroad, 65
Turkey, 42
Turkmenistan, 43
Tuvalu, 47

U
Uganda, 46
Ukraine, 40
underground railways, 65
UNESCO, 35
United Arab Emirates, 44
United Kingdom, 40
United Nations (UN), 35
United States of America, 38
  presidents, 52
  states, 48–9
Universe, 12–17
Uranus, 16–17
Uruguay, 39
Uzbekistan, 43

V
Vanuatu, 47
Vatican City, 42
Venezuela, 39
Venus, 16
Vietnam, 43
vitamins, 84
volcanoes, 28–9

volume, 97, 98

W
waltz, 118
wars, 58–9
water, 26–7
water speed records, 100, 101
waterfalls, 27
wavelengths, 82–3
weight, 97, 98
Western Samoa, 47
wheat, 51
White House, 49
wind speeds, 101
Winter Olympic Games, 112
world:
  climate zones, 30–1
  Earth's crust, 28–9
  map, 36–37
  night sky, 12–13
  physical world, 24–5
  planet Earth, 18–21
  sun and moon, 14–15
  time zones, 22–3
  water, 26–7
World Health Organization
  (WHO), 35
world organizations, 35
writing, 108–9

Y
Yemen, 43

Z
Zaire, 44
Zambia, 45
Zimbabwe, 45
Zoroastrianism, 111

Acknowledgements

Dorling Kindersley would like to thank:
Hilary Bird for the index; Louise Cox for design assistance; the Science Museum; Caroline Potts for picture library services; Chris Jackson and Dave Roberts for cartographic assistance.

Illustrations by:
Russell Barnett, Richard Blakely, Richard Bonson, Peter Bull, Kuo Kang Chen, Luciano Corbella, Brian Delf, William Donohue, Eugene Fluery, Roy Flookes, Bob Garwood, Will Giles, Mike Grey, Nick Hall, Nick Hewetson, Colette Ho, Bruce Hogarth, John Hutchinson, Richard Lewis, Mick Loates/Linden Artists, Judith Maguire, Janos Marfy, Kate Miller, Richard Platt, Sandra Pond, Sabastian Quigley, J. Robins, Colin Rose, Colin Salmon, Rodney Shackell, Roger Stewart, John Temperton, Richard Ward, John Woodcock.

Photographs by:
Peter Chadwick, Geoff Dann, Philip Dowell, Mike Dunning, Peter Hayman, Chas Howson, Gary Kevin, Dave King, Neil Lukas, Eric Meacher, Ray Moller, Steve Oliver, Dave Rudkin, Kim Sayer, Clive Steeter, Jane Stockman.

Picture credits:
The publisher would like to thank the following for their kind permission to reproduce their photographs:

t=top b=bottom c=centre l=left r=right.
© Acadamy of Motion Picture Arts and Sciences ®: 116 br; British Museum: 56 l; Bureau Internationale des Poids et Mesures, Sèvres: 96 cl; Corbis/ Bettman/ UPI: 115 cl; Eurostar/ European Passenger Services/ de Souza: 65 tl; Mary Evans Picture Library: 120 br; Glasgow Museums/ The Burrell Collection: 121 t ; The Ronald Grant Archive: Lawnmower Man/ First Independent Films Ltd 73 tl; Robert Harding Picture Library: 49 tl, Nigel Francis 38 tl, 60–61, Adam Woolfit 102–103; IBM: 72 bl; The Image Bank: George Obremski 52 tl, Harald Sund 53 br, Terry Williams 66 cl, Imperial War Museum: 59 tr; © The Henry Moore Foundation: Michael Muller 115 br; Museum of Artillery: 58 tl; NASA: 13 tr,14 l, 15 tl, 18 bl, 18 cl, 77 br; Rex Features Ltd: Patrick Frilet 51 br; Tony Stone Images: 100 tl; United Nations: 32–33; Wallace Collection: 58 r

Every effort has been made to trace the copyright holders and we apologize in advance for any unintentional omissions. We would be pleased to insert the appropriate acknowledgement in any subsequent edition of this publication.